A Walk To Gethsemane, Touching The Master

Linda J Humes

Published by Linda J Humes, 2024.

While every precaution has been taken in the preparation of this book, the publisher assumes no responsibility for errors or omissions, or for damages resulting from the use of the information contained herein.

A WALK TO GETHSEMANE, TOUCHING THE MASTER

First edition. February 14, 2024.

Copyright © 2024 Linda J Humes.

ISBN: 979-8224035120

Written by Linda J Humes.

Table of Contents

A Walk
To
Gethsemane
~ Touching the Master's Hand ~

By Linda J. Humes

PROLOGUE

There are times when we seek God for wisdom for a situation. There are times when we cry out to God in intercession for a loved one. There are times when we humbly kneel before God for peace over our circumstances. Then there are times when we quietly sit, talk, praise and meditate on His Holy Word. Times when we intimately share with God our true appreciation for His precious daily gifts.

It is during these precious, intimate times that God tenders our hearts to hear His loving voice. During those moments we are touched with inspiration and the revelation of His greatness. These are times when we join the Master on "A Walk To Gethsemane.

This book is dedicated to those moments and the wisdom He has shared during those many walks. Find a quiet place, begin with prayer and enjoy the tender words of hope inspired by A Walk To Gethsemane.

Friends

"A man that hath friends must show himself friendly: and there is a friend that sticketh closer than a brother." Proverbs 18:24

When I was happy,
You rejoiced with me.
When I was troubled,
You listened.
When I was sad,
You shared my tears.
When I saw despair for tomorrow,
You reminded me of yesterday.
When I saw hopelessness,
You turned my face toward Jesus.
Thank you for being . . .
My Friend.

A Moment in Time

"And ye shall know the truth, and the truth shall make you free." John 8:32

Satan takes a moment in time,
and creates a most horrible incident,
that scars and fractures,
our views and beliefs,
for the rest of our lives.
He strategically places in our path,
demonized souls – the mentally ill,
some that say that they come,
in the name of the Lord,
to steal our innocence,
fill us with fear,
and distort the way we view,
every person, every sound,
every surrounding, every shape,
every race, every fragrance,
from that day forward.
We cower consciously for months or years,
subconsciously for decades,
trying to walk past the anxieties,
we may not understand.
We displace the anger and hurt onto the innocent,
often onto those people we love the most,
justifying our behavior with false truths,
and attempting Biblical justification,
but knowing deep inside,

our actions were wrong,
yet not knowing how to stop,
and feeling deeper and deeper guilt,
because of it.
We blame God for not being there,
we run from the very presence,
that can bring us healing.
We run from others,
we run from ourselves,
we run from every possible circumstance,
that could possibly bring us pain.
We run and run and run,
until we are unable to take,
another step.
It's at that moment,
when we can run no farther,
when we cry out to others for answers,
when we cry out to God for help,
that Jesus can draw close.
It's in that time that we can see,
that He was with us,
all the time,
crying with our pain,
holding us as we wept in the night,
waiting for us to call upon Him,
to heal the brokenness,
we can no longer endure.
In that breaking moment,
when Satan's shackles are broken away,
when our mind is refreshed,
and our vision restored,
that healing comes,

wave by wave,
washing, cleansing, renewing.
Prejudice is lost,
fear is captured,
hatred is banished,
anger subdued,
life restored.
Come Lord Jesus.

Turning Around

"Be still, and know that I am God: . . ." Psalm 46:10
I have never known the love of a natural Father.
But through the unconditional love of my children,
You have shown me how precious it can be.
I have found it so very hard to trust man,
But You have shown me that love can be present,
Without performance or expectation.
I have struggled through past loneliness,
But You have shown me the treasure of being alone,
And quiet before You.
Thank You for turning my world around.

A Pocket Full of Miracles

"Pray without ceasing." 1 Thessalonians 5:17

". . . The effectual fervent prayer of a righteous man availeth much."
James 5:16

All of my life I've had a terrible habit that I haven't been able to break. My mother always lets me know how unladylike it is – and I agree – I just can't stop! No matter how hard I try, I just can't keep my hands out of my pockets.

Over the years I've lost my ability to remember things (even my name once or twice). To compensate for my memory "challenge", I have been known to write myself notes and stuff them in my pockets. Sometimes the notes prove useful, but most of the time they get wadded and creased and become illegible by the time I truly need them.

One day, while browsing through a Christian Bookstore (my very favorite pastime), I came upon "A Cross In My Pocket" coins and medals. They come in several shapes and sizes. I began to search for five separate medals, each with its own special purpose. Before long I had found just what I wanted – the miracles had begun.

The largest coin has a cross on the front with "Dad" engraved over the top. On the back is a prayer of thanksgiving for who he is. This coin would represent my husband. With a silent prayer I slipped him into my pocket.

The next largest coin says "Jesus" across the front and it cites a scripture on the back. It is the heaviest coin and represents my heaviest burden at this time, my teenage son. So easily he could turn the wrong way, yet through prayer and intercession I have faith that he will remain on the right path. With a silent prayer I slipped him into my pocket.

Next comes a nickel with a cross stamped out of the center. It was new and shiny, and the perfect coin to represent my 9-year-old son who has not yet shown an interest in drawing close to the cross. With a prayer I slipped him into my pocket, along with the other two.

Next is a coppery penny with a heart stamped out of the center. This is the coin, which represents my 7-year-old son. This is a child abundantly filled with a love of God. This is a child that will, one day, help the broken-hearted heal from their wounds. With a prayer he was slipped into my pocket.

The last coin is a light aluminum coin with a cross on one side and the "Cross In My Pocket" story on the other. This coin represents the special needs of the people of the church. One day it represented my two youngest sons' birth mother, the next day an ill friend, and the next an evangelist with a special prayer request. This coin changes daily, yet it rests in the closeness of my pocket, in covenant with the prayers for my family.

This is my pocket full of miracles. Every time I thrust my hand down into my pocket I feel the coins and I begin to pray. I caress each coin, identify the shape and design with my fingers, and say a special prayer as I hold them.

Like the bit of sand that irritates and festers in the shell of the oyster, the small metal coins that fill my pocket, and jingle as I walk, will bring forth a precious gift, more beautiful than a pearl, in miraculous answered prayer.

What a small price to pay to always be reminded of those people I love, dozens of times a day, and offer up specific prayers to guide their precious lives.

Lord, remind me daily that I can never pray too often for the wonderful people you've placed in my life. And, even though I may never see the answer to all of those prayers, may I always remember that You have the answers in the palm of Your hand, and that you will release them when the moment is right.

Stone Bruise

Be still, and know that I am God: I will be exalted among the heathen, I will be exalted in the earth. Psalm 46:10

We often fall into sin by such small degrees, that we don't realize where we are or how we got there. It's much like having a pebble in your shoe. It's a little uncomfortable, and you wish it wasn't there, but not enough to stop and remove the pebble, taking precious time to loosen the laces and shake the shoe out. Instead, we wiggle or shake our foot and move the annoyance to the side where it doesn't hurt - at least not with every step. Once in a while it gets right under your heel and stops you cold in your steps, but only for a moment. With a quick shake it moves to the side and you're off again.

Sin befalls us that way, too. It starts in our life as something that makes us a little uncomfortable, but we shake it to the side and let it be. Every once in a while it stands up and stares us in the face, but we move it aside again and convince ourselves that it isn't big enough to take the time to remove. Only, it never really goes away - it's still there, just in a less bothersome place. And the effects of it grow greatly when we bruise our heel or little toe - then it becomes more and more distractive - yet, at the same time, it becomes more and more familiar. And even though it can be quite uncomfortable, we know we would miss the little annoyance that gives us thought throughout the day. After all, it's just a little pebble. We can toss it out any time we want. Or can we?

Chrysalis

"Wherefore, if God so clothe the grass of the field, which today is, and tomorrow is cast into the oven, shall he not much more clothe you, O ye of little faith?" Matthew 6:30

I made a new friend the other day. He wasn't attractive - didn't have a "big" name - wasn't famous; in fact, he didn't have anything to do with the church! Yet, Jesus, he taught me more - about you - than the most eloquent, the most learned, person I've heard.

My little friend - short and plump - rested briefly on a tomato stem, preparing to consume yet another leaf. This little caterpillar - subjected daily to the mercies of his environment - was bound to the earth by those areas where he could climb.

He was so perfectly made - just like you - just like me. Every curve, every stout little leg, every perfect oval marking, balanced and ordered by a meticulous God.

He pressed forward, eating intently, knowing that soon he must die, and resting in the faith, that in his death he will be born again. He will soon take his earth-bound body, wrap it carefully in instinctive faith, and wait for the day when he will soar with a new freedom - as a beautiful, delicate butterfly.

We, too, can make the decision to wrap up our earth-bound lives and dispose of the old self, allowing the freeing release of the Holy Spirit, giving us wings to soar into the Presence of God.

The caterpillar, in his instinctive faith, never wastes a moment wondering "if" - he is drawn to the freedom he KNOWS will come. Oh, that we could have the faith to shed all that binds us to the ground. That we might wrap ourselves completely in the chrysalis of the Word of God, pulled tight by the power of the Spirit that transforms us. That we would desire to be drawn to that freedom - unafraid of the heights that we could soar to - through the rebirth from our old self to Christ.

Quiet Place

"My righteousness is near; my salvation is gone forth, and mine arms shall judge the people; the isles shall wait upon me, and on mine arm shall they trust." Isaiah 51:5

Gathered in His arms, resting In His lap.

A daughter held safely in the tender arms of her Father.

We rock gently, back and forth,

To the song You've placed in my heart.

The warmth of love radiates through me.

It is a preciousness I feel nowhere else.

And as the pressures of the day begin to push in,

I will step away to a quiet place.

I will wrap Your arms around me,

And taste the sweetness of Your love,

That burns always in my heart.

Crimson Blood

*Now the God of peace, that brought again from the dead our Lord
Jesus, that great shepherd of the sheep, through the blood of the
everlasting covenant, Hebrews 13:20*

So curious a creature are we,
ingenious in the ways of war,
yet perplexed by wounds,
ever so greater,
than any weapon,
could ever conceive.
Wounds so deep,
into the hearts,
of our smallest children,
that no medicine made,
today or tomorrow,
could ever lift the pain,
piercing through.
Fatal wounds inflicted,
by those they love most,
in acts of anger,
in acts of arrogance,
in tearing away,
from the gift they call love.
When the hope dies,
along with worthiness,
the wounded child,

remains small,
though the body may grow,
to adulthood,
to accountability.
Where, then, do they turn,
when they scream out for love,
from a deadened heart,
pushed so deeply,
into a box,
of protective devices,
flushed by deadening tasks?
Who, then, can see,
into the callused eyes,
shielding the soul,
from any possibility,
of additional wounds.
Only the Son of Light,
can burn so bright,
as to see into the depths,
of a lightless life.
Only the Son of Life,
can loosen the sword,
of tainted love,
and killing words,
to free the fatal wound,
in the deadened heart,
of a little child,
now the shape of a man.
It is only the Son,
who called us from birth,
set angels at our side,
and prayed with our prayers,

until the day,
we were ready to heal.
It is only the Son,
who's dark crimson blood,
entered into the wound,
lubricating the weapon,
only He could remove,
cauterizing the opened cavity,
filling it with the endless gift,
of God's perfect love.

The Dance of Creation

"In the beginning God created the heaven and the earth." Genesis 1:1

In the beginning there was God.

They lived there – in eternity. God the Father, God the Son, God the Holy Ghost. One in three, three in one, which was, and is, and is to come.

Within them dwelt all good things – joy and peace, and so much love. Such loss to have so much and have no one to share it with.

A delightful thought! Oh, what bliss. A kingdom, a nation, seed of seed, Paradise!

The thought welled up inside of them. Excitement filled their hearts. One would be Heaven, one would be Earth.

"Yes, Yes," smiled God. "A Heaven and an Earth."

Into being He called them, and they were. There, like the potter's clay, waiting – desolate – empty – void. Waiting in darkness to be formed and shaped. The very depths of heaven and earth lay still – expecting.

Down came the breath of God, fluttering across the face of the waters. The living waters, the catalyst of all things to come. Sent abroad by God the Holy Spirit, one day to be released in all living things. One day to be released into you, into me.

Then God spoke into the waters, "Let there be light."

The joy of God rose up, bright and clear, lighting the heaven, lighting the earth. It was a good thing.

The brightness of His joy shown greatly. Yes, it was good.

Yet, who would know light if there was no darkness, or darkness if there was no light? Joy if there was no emptiness, emptiness if there was no joy?

Up God stood, creating He both, one side darkness, one side light. Separate, one from the other. The light rested at His right hand. He called the light Day. In His left hand He grasped the darkness. Twisting it away from the light. The darkness he called Night.

From the dusk of the evening, traveling into the darkness, to the dawn of the new morning, coming safely out of the darkness, was the first day.

————-

Ah, yes, it had begun. It was the beginning of time – the first strokes from the Master's palette.

Filled with excitement God began to dance. Around and around He spun, laughing and dancing. He reached out with His mighty arm and cut through the waters as He spun about.

"Let there be a firmament in the midst of the waters. Let it divide the waters from the waters."

As he spun the waters above pulled up high, carving the giant arch of the sky. The waters below remained level, trembling as He danced, swelling with the music that played within Him, receding with the peace within the Master's soul, knowing all was well.

There they danced together, the Father, the Son, the Holy Spirit, and the waters of the sky He called heaven. There they danced.

From the dusk of the evening, traveling into the darkness, to the dawn of the new morning, coming safely out of the darkness, it was now the second day.

————

There stood He – there stood they – enjoying the fruits of His dance. As far as the eye could see, as far as the mind could imagine, there rose the sky. Painted royal blue, pure and clear.

Searching the waters below the heaven, God began to leap as He danced.

"Let the waters under the heaven be gathered together into one place, and let the dry land appear."

The land had patiently waited for its time. Now, with every setting down of His foot the land pushed up from below. Joyfully He danced. Joyfully He laughed. The breath of His laughter blew upon the rising land and it dried as it rose, taking shape.

As He danced and rejoiced the mountains climbed to kiss the hem of His garment, then rose again to meet the hem of the sky. The hills and valleys made their place, and the waters gathered together in the lowest places.

The dry land called He Earth and the gathered waters called He Seas. There forever to stand, hand in hand, to prepare the Eden to come. They reached back and forth, grasping strength, one from the other, flowing together over the subtle boundaries appointed to them.

God watched and smiled. It was good.

Once again He began to dance, scattering visions of abundance upon the new earth.

"Let the earth bring forth grass, the herb yielding seed, and the fruit tree yielding fruit after its kind, whose seed is in itself, upon the earth."

And even as He spoke the fragile blades pushed through the new land of this place called earth. Up rose the grass, the herb, the trees and the bushes – each with the seed to bring new life, inside its tender flower.

Up rose the fruit tree, with sweet tender fruit, kissed by the laughter of God as He saw the beauty of its bough, and knew of the pleasures and blessings it would bring to those yet to come.

Quickly it grew and budded and bloomed, dropping its precious seed to birth and grow and multiply. Precious plants of different species and gifts. Each needing another of its own kind to pollinate the buds of the new plants to come. Each species with a seed of its own, to bear its own kind, again and again and again. Each brought forth with a special purpose, a special need to meet, all a precious part of the vision God saw.

Nothing laid waste. Nothing was set without a plan. Everything was perfectly fitted together.

From the dusk of the evening, traveling into the darkness, to the dawn of the new morning, coming safely out of the darkness, this was the third day.

———————

As He tipped back His head God gave a shout of laughter. He spread His arms wide and cherished the great dome called heaven.

"Let there be lights in the firmament of the heaven to divide the day from the night; and let them be for signs, and for seasons, and for days, and years: And let them be for lights in the firmament of the heaven to give light upon the earth."

As He stood, arms wide, a glow grew from within Him and spread all about. No longer could the edge of light and the edge of darkness be seen, but one flowed and melted into the other, slowly, gently.

Into His right hand He blew and there grew a great light. Casting it deep into the heaven, it took its place high into the light. This was the light appointed to govern the day.

Into His left hand He blew and a lesser light formed. He cast it deep into the heaven and it went high into the darkness. This was the light appointed to govern the night.

He cupped His hands together and blew within. A glow danced between His palms, illuminating the beauty of His presence. Casting them out He scattered the stars far into the depths of the firmament. Deep into this place called heaven. There they shown brightly against the darkness of night. Some shown so bright that they could even be seen through the light of day.

These lights, great and small, were set precisely in the firmament, assigned to make a light upon the earth. Proudly in their places, they received their appointment with greatest honor - to govern the day, to govern the night, and to separate the light from the darkness.

God watched as they began the purpose they were ordained for. Resting in the heaven; watchful, strong, sure. The warmth of the greater light caressed His face.

"Yes," God nodded, it was good.

From the dusk of the evening, traveling into the darkness, to the dawn of the new morning, coming safely out of the darkness, this was the fourth day.

———————

Down He knelt and touched the waters with His hand. As He raised it to His lips the waters trickled down His arm. Deep He looked into the water, then around at the dry land. He stood and scanned the horizon of trees; now fully grown, fruitful, preparing to drop precious seeds.

"Let the waters bring forth abundantly the moving creature that hath life, and fowl that fly above the earth in the open firmament of heaven." With the vibration of His mighty voice the waters began to tremble and shake. Within the vibration grew a vibration. Swarming, creeping, growing - new life in the depths of the waters. From the smallest invertebrate to the giant whale, each in schools of its own species, there grew the first life.

And as the sea swelled with the abundance of new birth, birds filled the boughs of the trees and soared against the blue of heaven. Each species resting within its own species, immediately starting the cycle of new life.

"Yes," it was good.

As He knelt there He blessed them, all that had come.

"Be fruitful and multiply, and fill the waters in the seas, and let fowl multiply in the earth.

From the dusk of the evening, traveling into the darkness, to the dawn of the new morning, coming safely out of the darkness, this was the fifth day.

———————

The birds painted the sky with the graceful strokes of their wings. They sang praises to the Master, Father God. The skies were filled with their anthem chorus. The great whales and the dolphins echoed back their own song of worship. The earth was alive with rejoicing.

"Let the earth bring forth the living creature after its kind, cattle, and creeping thing, and beast of the earth after his kind," said God.

There, from the bushes, the caverns, and the trees walked the fruits of new life. Each with its own kind, each in harmony with the other. The great beasts and the small. The reptiles and the rodents. All taking their place in the cycle of life. Each recognizing their need for the other.

The lion and the lamb lay at His feet. The truth of the moment, the truth of Eden, a prophesy of a day to come.

God tarried there, enjoying the moment of innocence. Cherishing what had become. He saw that it was good.

"Let us make man in our image, after our likeness: and let them have dominion over the fish of the sea, and over the fowl of the air, and over the cattle, and over all the earth, and over every creeping thing that creepeth upon the earth."

Sitting upon a rock God leaned forward and scooped together the warm soil. He raised His hands up and allowed the powdery soil to trickle through His fingers. Moving left to right, right to left, the soil fell to the ground.

As it touched the face of the earth it began to move and take shape. An arm, a leg, the torso, the head. Down upon it God blew, moving the powdery residue away from the new creation.

He lifted this man from the cradle of his birth and blew into his face. The man gasped his first breath and opened his eyes - looking innocently into the face of God. Out of the dirt grew bone and muscle, blood and sinew. Out of the earth came love and joy, long-suffering and gentleness. Out of the soil came man, created in the image of God, resembling Him in feature and form.

With the guiding strength of God's hand man stood and surveyed the land that God had appointed him to rule. He did not fear the vastness, he did not fear the task of naming and ruling and subduing all that had been created. But he did fear the times of loneliness in those times when God was not walking with him or talking to him. He had so much to share.

God felt the man's loneliness, his sadness, his pain, and he brought to man woman. Created by God, out of man. Bone of his bone, blood of his blood, a woman to share all of his days.

As the knelt, hand in hand, man and woman, at the feet of God, He blessed them and said unto them, "Be fruitful and multiply, and replenish the earth, and subdue it: and have dominion over the fish of the sea, and over the fowl of the air, and over every living thing that moveth upon the earth."

"Behold, I have given you every herb bearing seed, which is upon the face of the earth, and every tree, in the which is the fruit of a tree yielding seed; to you it shall be for meat. And to every beast of the earth, and to every fowl of the air, and to everything that creepeth upon the earth, wherein there is life, I have given every green herb for meat."

Man and woman turned and beheld all that God had given them. Every creature, great and small, ate of the green herb and grasses that grew. Every fish, every fowl, every mammal ate of the same food. There was no fear, there was no danger, only appointed positions to which God had called them.

This was the land that man and woman were to call into order, by the grace of God. These were the seas that would carry the precious life that could only survive in the waters. This was the heaven and earth they were to rule and reign over. This was their home.

Hand in hand they walked away from the glorious presence of God and into the land before them. God watched as the creatures of the sea, the fowl of the air and the creatures of the land humbled themselves before the two called man and woman. He saw them warmed by the sun and caressed by the herbs beneath their feet. The sky crowned their heads and the flowers of the land adorned them.

"Yes," thought God. It was VERY good.

From the dusk of the evening, traveling into the darkness, to the dawn of the new morning, coming safely out of the darkness, this was the sixth day.

———

There stood God, in the midst of them. He gazed far to the east, then deep into the west. He turned and searched north and then again south. Slowly He turned, around and around, not wanting to miss the slightest blessing.

It was finished. The heavens, the earth, the creatures above, the creatures below, and those that walked the land. It was finished. Creation.

On this day, the seventh day, God rested. He savored the breeze and the warmth of the sun. He cherished the rich green grass beneath His feet, and the water that caressed His hands as He dipped them. He revered man and woman and the moments they would share as they walked the paths of Eden in the cool of the evening.

He memorized the cut of the mountain and the velvet of the hills. With fatherly pride He watched as each creature walked and dwelt in harmony, submitted to those made in His image.

It was finished. The dance of creation had come to a close. The staccato of the music mellowed to a sweet aria.

He sat and enjoyed this world He had created - and He rested. Such peace. This day, the last day of creation, God blessed above all others and He sanctified it.

This day would be the day, throughout all of the generations, that would be set aside, dedicated and holy. A day each week for that special intimate communion with the one true God.

And this was the order of creation. This was the generation of the heaven and the earth. This was the plan that God set into motion for the world before us. This was new life. THIS WAS GOOD.

The Mother

"... how often would I have gathered thy children together, as a hen doth gather her brood under her wings..." Luke 13:34

A belt of Gold brings together
A Garment of Praise -
Purple and Azure -
And a covering of Righteousness
White and Pure.
A Crown of Royalty rests on her Head -
Wrapped in Purple,
Yet unadorned,
For the Wedding Day has not yet come.
Majestic Arms,
Strong and Firm,
Reach out to the Nations,
Then gather back together the wounded and grieved,
In a warm embrace.
Standing firm,
On a strong foundation,
Not gilded or adorned with useless jewelry,
Set soundly on a true doctrine,
That none may cover.
She pours out the sustenance needed,
To strengthen the Saints of God.
One vessel holding the Priest's share of the sacrifices,
Brought to the Brazen Altar,

Given graciously to those who hunger.
One vessel holds the precious food of the Spirit,
The Word of God,
Served to build the body of faith.
Eyes keenly upon the task at hand,
Not to the left or the right.
Face radiant with the glory of God,
Anointed to shepherd the people,
Those unwanted by the church of glass and velvet,
Those needing the foundation and guidance,
To heal.

The hand of the 5-fold ministry,
Carefully pours the anointing out,
To those appointed to fulfill the need.
The Mother,
The Church,
Will rise,
Bearing the vessels of truth and righteousness,
On its shoulders,
Looking for a people, to dip and drink.
It will rise in strength and confidence,
Knowing her place.
Only setting her work aside,
For a moment,
That moment when she embraces her children,
Blessing them and sending them forward,
To find their place.
Then lifting her vessels again,
Placing them firmly upon her shoulders,
She presses onward.

Eden

"The Lord God hath given me the tongue of the learned, that I should know how to speak a word in season to him that is weary: he wakeneth morning by morning, he wakeneth mine ear to hear as the learned." Isaiah 50:4

It's late. Everyone is finally off to their own rooms, preparing to sleep; some are already successful. I head for my quiet spot, the master bathroom. It's very small, built for usefulness, not flair. With the door closed, as it will (which is almost), all the lights on and the exhaust fan rattling out the household noises that remain, it is my only refuge. There I read and write and pray and listen for God.

Before too long a paw reaches under the door and pulls it open enough for one (or more) of my cats to come in. At first they are content to lap at the water dripping from the faucet, soon curling up in the oval shaped sink, lightly dozing. Most of the time they wait patiently for me to finish, but on occasion they will try tenaciously to get onto my lap for hugging and petting, sending books and Bibles, pens and paper flying. Giving in is the best defense, fighting back by trying to chase them off creates a greater distraction than taking a few minutes to love on them. They so desperately want to please, having no idea that they are in the least bit annoying. Soon, I set them back down, retrieve my papers and books and go back to praying and listening - and hoping once again to be anointed and used by God.

There are times when I've wished I could remain there for days, but responsibility calls. I have spent many wonderful hours there, in communion, not wanting to leave. Fatigue and worry escape me there – as does time, sometimes putting my night's sleep at risk.

It's just a bathroom, with its own white noise and its own bright light, generally shared with several purring cats, waiting contently in the sink – but to me it becomes Eden. A place where I go to seek the face of God and talk with Him in the cool of the evening. It's there that I remember to thank God for the little things that He does to show me His love.

I thank Him, that even in the inner city, without a natural setting to run to, I have a bathroom, big enough to hold one small bookcase and lots of pens and paper. I thank Him that I have cats who remind me to always take time for a hug and a kind word. And I thank Him for the understanding that no matter where I am, God will be there to meet me.

Stand Back

"And all this assembly shall know that the LORD saveth not with
sword and spear: for the battle is the Lord's, and he will give you into
our hands." 1 Sam 17:47

I say stand back, stand back, in the Lord.
Egypt's Red Sea seemed a mighty foe.
With Pharaoh close there seemed no place to go.
The people stood and cried aloud with fear.
Forgetting all along their Lord was there.
I say stand back, stand back in the Lord.
His mighty hand can move the sea from shore to shore.
I say stand back, stand back in the Lord.
Shielded by Armor of Faith we'll stand.
Jericho was girded all around,
A mighty fortress set on solid ground.
If rushed the army within would abound,
By marching feet and trumpets it went down.
Gideon was sent to take the land,
With only three hundred men he had to stand.
With pitchers, lanterns, horns, he did God's will,
Though all the enemy died, he did not kill.
I say stand back, stand back in the Lord.
His mighty hand can move the sea from shore to shore.
I say stand back, stand back in the Lord.
Shielded by Armor of Faith we'll stand.
Deborah sent her army off to war,
The army would not go without her near,
The chariots of iron saved not the foe,

For God provided the rain, they moved no more.
Joshua was sent to take Ai,
To win this one he must be very sly.
Place armies front and back, came God's reply,
And hold your spear up high, high in the sky.
I say stand back, stand back in the Lord.
His mighty hand can move the sea from shore to shore.
I say stand back, stand back in the Lord.
Shielded by Armor of Faith we'll stand.
Do you have an enemy today?
Take your troubles to God, get down and pray,
There is nothing He can't rise above,
He's there to raise you up in perfect love.
I say stand back, stand back in the Lord.

Firewall

"That the trial of your faith, being much more precious than of gold
that perisheth, though it be tried with fire, might be found unto praise
and honour and glory at the appearing of Jesus Christ:" 1 Peter 1:7
In the eye of the storm,
The flame of faith,
Flickers and dims,
Holding perilously,
To yesterday's truths;
Praying.
Satan's doubt,
Quenches the flame,
Reducing it to an ember,
As the storm tarries.
A cry for help,
Faint, but heard.
Then, in a moment,
The flame surges,
Grows, strengthens,
When joined by the faith,
Of interceding saints,
Building a firewall,
Of committed prayer,
That banishes doubt,
And fuels the flame,
With the testimony of miracles.
Stand with me,
When the cutting winds blow,

Then I will be strengthened,
And ready to join with you,
When another saint's flame,
Begins to dim.

Changes

"But blessed are your eyes, for they see: and your ears, for they hear."
Matthew 13:16

Life races by in a smattering of light and noise,

Glimpses of love and warmth stir past.

How could I have missed the changes?

Oh, to stand still and recognize the fragrance of time.

To linger long enough to be refreshed in a spring rain.

To notice that flowers grow wild in a field.

Help me, Lord, to stop and see,

The simple treasures,

You've given to me.

Generations

"Thou shalt not bow down thyself to them, nor serve them: for I the Lord thy God am a jealous God, visiting the iniquity of the fathers upon the children unto the third and fourth generation of them that hate me;" Exodus 20:5

"Thou shewest lovingkindness unto thousands, and recompensest the iniquity of the fathers into the bosom of their children after them: the Great, the Mighty God, the Lord of hosts, is his name," Jeremiah 32:18

The weight of the sins,
of generations past,
burden my shoulders.
I am tempted and swayed,
toward an evil I don't understand,
and yet I crave.
I carry the mantle of a cursed generation,
passed down,
father to child,
a covenant of sin.
In which generation do I fall,
3rd, 5th, maybe 7th?
The shadow of a cross
falls across the path,
I've been destined to walk.
It breaks the pulling of the grave.
As I look to the man hanging there,
calling my name,
I feel the mantle lighten.

Resting at His feet,
I look upward,
into His pain wracked face;
the blood from His pierced hands,
falls on the mantle I carry,
breaking the chains that hold it there,
releasing the shell,
it falls to the ground.
His eyes watch and question,
"Will you pick it back up?"
Within my womb rests a nation.
Their destiny rests within the choice,
I must make.
Their blessing or cursing
rests in the power
of my decision.
Do I pick up the mantle
of my fathers,
or wear a crown of thorns,
adorned with the ruby red drops
of the Savior's blood,
one day to be traded
for a crown of gold.
There, at the foot of the cross,
lay the empty shell,
a wicked generation
left behind - cleansed
by the flow of blood.

The Day The Angels Cried

"And Jesus answered him, The first of all the commandments is, Hear, O Israel; The Lord our God is one Lord: [30] And thou shalt love the Lord thy God with all thy heart, and with all thy soul, and with all thy mind, and with all thy strength: this is the first commandment. [31] And the second is like, namely this, Thou shalt love thy neighbour as thyself. There is none other commandment greater than these." Mark 12:29-31

September 11th, 2001 will be one of those dates that no one will forget. It has engraved its importance upon our spirits and hangs heavy in our memory. September 11th, 2001 was the day the angels cried.

No one will forget the horror of the airplanes bursting through the tower walls of the world trade center, or the empty helplessness of watching the men and women falling the 80 to 90 stories to the ground. We felt hope as we watched the fire, police and rescue personnel head into the chaos and devastation when the towers swallowed them up.

When we saw the 110-story towers implode and disintegrate into powdery dust, dust made from concrete and glass, snowing down in a suffocating blizzard, we were there. Who the dust covered people were wasn't important. The race, creed or color of the person wasn't important. They were life - that was important. They were family - brothers and sisters who's names we may never know, who's stories we may never hear, but they were family - tied to us by the horror of the breach of freedom we so generously share.

America. A country so tender that we sat for hours glued to a TV screen and prayed, encouraged and cheered when rescue workers freed baby Jessica McClure from an abandoned well. A country so generous that we open our arms to the thousands of immigrants who cross our borders every year - providing them food, shelter, medical care and education. A country so strong that after wars and conflicts, we have been able to return home and raise our families with humility and a sense of forgiveness and peace. A blessed country, graciously blessing others. A country betrayed.

America. The tenderness and generosity grievously stunned by such a horrific act. America. Attacked strategically to destroy our economy and military intelligence - but rising up to recognize that in the moments of tragedy only one thing mattered - life and the preservation of it.

Helplessly scattered across the nation, we reached out with truckloads of food, clothing and medical supplies. We donated money from our household budgets to send to the Red Cross and Salvation Army who tended the victims and the rescue workers. We stood hours in line to give blood to send to the hospitals near ground zero. We mourn the deaths, rejoice with the miracles, encourage the jobless - and we pray. When we could do no more, we sat and watched the live news, for hours, days, weeks, and prayed; even still - we pray.

The probability of life in the wreckage is no longer. The fires that have burned in the stories of the crushed building for weeks send eerie symbolism of the bowels of Hell. Satan came down to destroy a country built on the premise of the Bible and dedicated to God, but he failed. What Satan has done to destroy America, God has turned around and created a new and wonderful understanding of what America is. God brought back to us the very foundations that this country was birthed on. God united the people and told the world that we are ONE. One people, one race, one color, one family - one AMERICA.

We will never forget the thousands entombed in the death of that majestic building - just as we have never forgotten the sailors entombed in the USS Arizona. In time we will forgive the misguided souls that did this - but we will never forget. Life will go on with some changes, but nothing that we, as individuals and as a nation, cannot overcome.

Since that day, the American people have been a little quieter; introspective. Mothers and fathers hold their children a little closer, holding their hands when they're in public. Trivial things don't matter anymore. People don't squabble in line at the grocery stores. Traffic is reduced, only traveling if necessary. The malls, restaurants and theatres are nearly empty where they used to be overflowing. People work less hours and spend more time with their families. We have become more aware of the treasures of life, and less caught up in the luxury available. We have re-established contact with distant family and old friends. Families are going back to church and re-establishing their relationship with their creator. People are more aware of the things around them and how very precious they are.

Satan took away the lives of 6000+ members of our family - and God showed us the way back to the true meaning of life. America - the land of the free, the home of the brave - family bound together by God. Victorious.

Many families now are seeing their children off to a war in a land where life has no meaning. A land where poverty is overwhelming and need is so great. A land where one man has orchestrated a gross evil that has marred their world. Some of those families are sending their children to the ultimate sacrifice, to ensure that their country is once again safe. Jesus, grant us the grace to see you at every turn, no matter what the daily outcome seems. Jesus, build our faith with each passing moment. And Jesus, give us the strength to forgive, and the power to overcome.

Compound Blessings

"And I say unto you, Ask, and it shall be given you; seek, and ye shall find; knock, and it shall be opened unto you." Luke 11:9

I hold a blessing,
In my hand,
It's real,
And sound,
And beautiful.
I could keep the blessing,
And treasure its virtue.
When it's done,
I will hold the memory,
Like a sweet fragrance.
I could release the blessing,
And let it fall into the hands,
Of someone near,
Someone who may recognize,
Its treasure,
Or may see it,
With abandon.
Or I could receive it,
And give it to you,
A perfect gift,
Nothing lacking,
Into the hand,
Of one who needs,
The very fragrance,
It unlocks.

If I keep it,
It will fade with age,
Beautifully and gracefully,
Evaporating.
If I let it loose,
It may become a blessing,
Or may die a sudden death,
Unappreciated and alone.
But if I give it to you,
Into the hand it was meant to go,
Then I too will share the blessing,
By watching you,
Enjoying the perfect purpose,
For what it was send to do.
I give it now,
To you.

God's Perfect Gift

"I am the rose of Sharon, and the lily of the valleys." Song 2:1
You came up,
out of the desert,
as a pure white rose,
born in a wilderness,
breathtakingly fragrant.
You stood for all that was true,
in a land without water,
in a world wroth with sin,
forged in pain.
People searched you out,
grasping at your petals,
a sweet scent to hold on to,
until only the stem remained,
circled about with thorns.
When it seemed to all,
that nothing was left,
You bloomed again,
as the Phoenix bird,
rising from the ashes,
lifted high above the crowd,
on an unfinished wooden cross.
In your final flower,
the new petals fell,
each bearing the name,
of sin and pain,
all that was removed,

from our condemned lives.
The petals falling,
willingly given,
to redeem the lost,
every provision considered,
every provision met.
First fell shame,
for not recognizing,
who You were,
then guilt,
for the pain You endured.
There was sickness,
depression, fear,
sins of the past,
broken in travel,
to the generations,
of the future.
On and on they fell,
one by one,
stripping away hopelessness,
giving new life,
in the sight of eternity.
As the last petal fell,
Your Father, our Father,
gasped,
shaking the earth with His pain,
dimming the light from the sky.
There You hung,
looking no more,
than a dry broken twig,
soon to be buried,
in the bowels of the earth.

Yet, inside that twig,
lay a seed,
a new life,
taking root in the earth,
preparing to grow,
preparing to bloom,
as Aaron's rod,
a sign to the nations,
of God's perfect love,
in the gift of,
the Rose.

Temptation

"There hath no temptation taken you but such as is common to man: but God is faithful, who will not suffer you to be tempted above that ye are able; but will with the temptation also make a way to escape, that ye may be able to bear it." 1 Corinthians 10:13

I gasp for air,
Shock electrifying my thoughts,
I have just seen the demon,
That torments my life.
Its reflection glanced past in a window glass,
And then another, and another.
I'm surrounded by the reality of it.
Can I pull free of the very evil that draws so near?
Do I have the strength to push away
The sin that feeds it?
I search my eyes in a mirror,
The demons stare back.
Come Holy Spirit and chase away,
The darkness that tries to hide within.
Be gone temptation,
Back to the recesses of time,
That I will sin no more.

Grace

"For the Lord God is a sun and shield: the Lord will give grace and
glory: no good thing will he withhold from them that walk uprightly."
Psalm 84:11

Ever so gently, the Spirit comes,
gently calling, gently waking,
the sleeping soul.
"Awake, Beloved, Arise,
join with me in sweet refreshing,
precious moments, you and I."
And though I try,
to fight the weariness,
I fall again,
to senseless sleep.
"Awake, Beloved, Arise,
rest in the peace only I can give."
My soul rocks,
battered by my own strengths,
by my own weaknesses.
The angels of light,
war with the angels of darkness,
fighting for the rights,
to my blessing.
Again I try to rise,
"Grace" - "Grace"
for spiritual strength,

to fight the demons,
that take their positions,
to stop the Rhema,
about to birth.
"Grace" - "Grace"
And with my cry,
a change begins,
a pounding pulse,
a surge of fire,
a rising up,
to the Spirit of truth.
In sweet communion,
with the one true Lord,
all weariness passes.
Refreshing of Spirit,
refreshing of soul,
no weakened limb,
just tender moments,
in anointed splendor.
"Arise, My Beloved,
and receive the gift,
I've so longed,
for you to have.
GRACE!

To Be 50

"Hearken unto thy father that begat thee, and despise not thy mother when she is old." Proverbs 23:22

Oh, what enjoyment to be 50.
At the stroke of midnight,
I went from rebellious to eccentric,
Opinionated to wise,
Distant to decisive.
I've seen the joy of a new century,
And remember the fear of nuclear fall-out.
Saw a man walk on the moon,
Which disproved a childhood belief,
That the moon was a ball of green cheese.
I've seen skirts go up, and down, and up again,
And pants that bell, then snuggle, and bell again.
I've started a life without TV
And now enjoy home theatre,
In my own living room.
I started with out-houses,
And ended up with 2 wonderful bathrooms,
One totally "Mickey" and one totally "Sports".
As long as the water continues to go down,
And not come back up,
They can stay in the house.
I've grown up to big bands,
Country/Western,
Folk Songs,
Rock & Roll,

And Rap.
I've heard it loud, I've heard it soft
– I prefer it soft.
I've seen my children born and grow,
Laugh and cry.
I've seen things that were once
So important to me,
Rest in boxes headed for a thrift shop.
I've found the value of a 2-hour nap,
And the treasure of eating out.
I still love reading a good book,
While sitting in front of a warm fire,
If it's winter.
A cool air conditioner,
If it's summer,
And out on the deck if it's spring.
Have I changed?
Maybe a little over the years.
But, I still wear Mickey Mouse shirts
And Eeyore overalls,
Have overindulged in surrounding myself
With pets,
Still treasure my family,
And covet my "free" time.
What has changed?
The way you look at me.
I slipped quietly into the next level of life,
And it made this wild ole' grandma acceptable,
With just the stroke of a clock.
Wouldn't it be wonderful to be accepted
Without having to grow old?

Grafted

"And they also, if they abide not still in unbelief, shall be grafted in: for God is able to graft them in again. For if thou wert cut out of the olive tree which is wild by nature, and wert grafted contrary to nature into a good olive tree: how much more shall these, which be the natural branches, be grafted into their own olive tree?" Romans 11:23-24

It was a deep wound,
Intended to bring death,
Inflicted by the spear,
Of a Roman Soldier.
Gaping open,
It released blood and water.
The blood of the new covenant,
The water of the Holy Spirit,
Yet to come.
The precious liquids,
Oozing to the surface,
Were the precious nutrients,
To give food and strength,
To the nation to come.
Inside that wound,
Deep in the side of my Savior,
The wound Satan meant for evil,
God planted a seed,
A bud,

A grafted nation,
A place for me.
That wound,
And the seed inside,
Were anointed with myrrh,
With aloes, and with spices.
Wrapped so carefully,
With the finest linen,
Preparing a cleft,
Of most Holy foundation,
For the Gentile to join,
God's chosen.
Then came the moment,
When the linens were left,
In the shape of a man,
But hollow and unaltered,
As a message of release.
The moment when Christ,
With the grafted children,
Tucked safely beneath his arm,
Faced Satan and conquered death.
Now this nation,
Birthed in the side of Christ,
As Eve was birthed,
In the side of Adam,
Sat in communion,
At the right hand of God.
Guided forth,
Performing greater miracles,
Exhibiting greater power,
Flowing in the Holy Spirit,
The seed branched forward.

Inside that graft,
With its roots entwined,
Deep into the Master,
There is a leaf,
Turning to the Son,
Preparing to break forth,
And follow the way,
Set forth by Him.
It's just one leaf,
Of the many branches,
Just one small part,
Of a mighty tree.
But on that leave,
Is a name,
And that name belongs,
To ME.

Your Love

"We love him, because he first loved us." 1 John 4:19

Lord, with the gentle fall of snow,
With the opening of a rose,
You have shown Your love for me.
Then, when the day has turned to night,
When the angels touch the sky,
You have shown Your love for me.
How could I ever doubt you're there,
With the wonders that we share,
Every day and everywhere.
Lord, keep me humble in my walk,
Let me teach as You have taught,
Show the world how much You care.

Harvest

"For all flesh is as grass, and all the glory of man as the flower of grass. The grass withereth, and the flower thereof falleth away: [25] But the word of the Lord endureth forever." 1 Peter 1:24-25

We grow each and every day. What we will be as we grow depends upon our parentage – how we will grow and develop depends on what we allow ourselves to be tended by.

Just as a flower, a rose will always produce a rose, a lily will produce a lily. But the strength and beauty of the plant is shaped by pure and plentiful water, as well as rich and fertile soil. A beautiful plant will wither and die without ever once producing a flower or seed when grown in a harsh dry area. A simple plant can become abundantly beautiful with special care, dropping its precious seed back into the soil as the flower dies, to produce again and again.

We make a choice - every day, every hour, every moment – as to the type of water we allow to be poured over our seed. We choose the stagnation of wicked thoughts and senseless gossip or the pure washing of the Word.

We make a choice of the ground that our seed will fall into. An arid desert where the children of Israel took 40 years to learn the greatness of God – and even then, only the children were allowed to cross over because the roots of the parents were broken off, but still firmly planted back in Egypt.

We make the choice of cultivating the soil with the rich blessings of God, as well as the truths and laws that give a firm foundation to support a healthy root. We make a choice.

Do we grasp our seed tightly in our hand so that no one else can get to it? Do we toss our seed casually aside, allowing it to fall where it will? Or do we place it carefully between our feet, to be guarded and tended until the day we must go on – and it remain.

The seed you hold is not for you. The seed you hold is not just one seed. The seed you hold is the seed of the seed it shall bear, and the seeds they shall bear, and the seeds they shall bear. Have you prepared for the harvest?

2 ½ Minutes - United

And the four beasts had each of them six wings about him; and they were full of eyes within: and they rest not day and night, saying, Holy, holy, holy, Lord God Almighty, which was, and is, and is to come. Revelation 4:8

On a recent vacation we traveled to California to visit family members not seen for too many years. The Northern California cultures and obvious lifestyle was such a change from our South Phoenix home.

We were completely overwhelmed by the large numbers of people at every turn. Traffic was bumper to bumper and lines at stores had to be a delight to the owners. Remarkably, we saw few confrontations because of these inconveniences, something I cannot brag about in our hometown. People there seemed to accept the inconvenience as a way of life, just the way things are.

Although I didn't notice outbursts of frustration, neither did I notice outbursts of pleasantries. People moved about much like ant colonies, each with a place to go and a job to do, no time to chitchat, no time to stop.

Shopping in San Francisco was an experience. When you weren't quick enough at choosing a souvenir in their overcrowded gift shops, someone would move over to assist you, pulling out articles from shelves, showing you hidden merchandise, color after color, then moving you quickly to the cash register line. I had to sit back and laugh at the adventure and wonder if we frustrated them as much as they frustrated us, all under the guise of a smile.

But of all the interesting things that happened, one 2-½ minute section of time touched me the most. On our way back from lunch with family we hadn't seen in 20 years, we decided to cross the Golden Gate Bridge.

Our boys had never seen the bridge and were excited as it began to come into view. They were blessed with the opportunity to study that bridge for quite a while, as we weren't the only family that had the idea. We sat, crawling, bumper to bumper, for miles before the bridge. My oldest son hung out the car window, snapping pictures of the bridge, Alcatraz Island, the city coastline, trees; you name it, anything to stay busy.

Not far from the bridge we had to pass through a tunnel. It was a tiled arched tunnel, marked and stained with age. I remembered the tunnel from my youth and the magic that seemed to spring to life as cars drove through – the lights passing by overhead and the long sounding honk as we swished under. Had it changed?

Almost as soon as we entered the tunnel the faces of the drivers began to change. First one car honked, then another. Three short bursts, followed by three more from another car – soon the tunnel swelled with an orchestra of patterns and phrases. People began to interact and play together, windows came down, laughter joined in, frustration left the faces of even the most distraught. For 2 ½ minutes they were children again, enjoying a moment of comradery with 50 complete strangers while creeping bumper to bumper in a tunnel – and enjoying every second of it.

All too soon the tunnel ended and the honking stopped, except for one lone car that would give 3 short bursts every once in a while, looking to see if anyone would join in outside of the tunnel – no one did.

As I reflected back I wondered if that experience might be a little bit like what Heaven is going to be? The cars will be replaced by white robes and the horns by voices. Instead of 3 short bursts of "beep, beep, beep" there will be long melodic arias of Holy, Holy, Holy. Every face will be happy, we will once again feel the joy of childhood and the safety of our Father's House.

Thank you Lord, for that glimpse of what treasures lie ahead. Thank you for a 2 ½ minute jewel today.

Hatred

"Whosoever hateth his brother is a murderer: and ye know that no murderer hath eternal life abiding in him." 1 John 3:15

Hatred, like a canker,
eats even to the most
tender part of the soul.
It rests at the edge of love,
volleying back and forth,
pretending to be one,
and then another.
It separates father and son,
brother and sister,
spirit and soul,
mind and body.
It lives by many names,
anger, jealousy, rage,
all dividing,
all destroying,
all pulling asunder,
that which once was one.
But whether it manifests
as rightful or wrongful,
it stands firm to one truth,
the end thereof is death.
Come, Sweet Jesus,
and purge this cancer,

that it will have no claim,
on this life I call Yours.

Revolution

For though we walk in the flesh, we do not war after the flesh: 4) (For the weapons of our warfare are not carnal, but mighty through God to the pulling down of strong holds;) 2 Corinthians 10: 4-3

Firmly we stand,
with pure hearts,
and cleansed souls,
fire coursing through our veins,
exuding the power,
of the anointing within.
Are you ready for a Revolution?
At battle status,
with sword and shield,
we take our positions,
as warring spirits,
in the battle ground,
for man's soul.
The army of God,
is cleansing a path,
for the graceful steps,
of the Bride of Christ.
No enemy can draw near,
no dart can reach its mark,
for the strength of David,
the wisdom of Deborah,
and the faith of John,
take authority,
over all principalities,

and powers of darkness.
Stand up, child of God,
renew your mind,
take your place,
as a Christian heir,
in the righteous army,
called to demand peace,
at all costs.
REVOLUTION!!

Humble Pastor Glen

(The Parable of the Little Red Hen)
Humble yourselves in the sight of the Lord, and he shall lift you up.
James 4:10

Once upon a time . . .

a Philosopher, a Bible Scholar, a Theologian, and Humble Pastor Glen, all dwelt together, in the same peaceful church.

The Philosopher liked to sit all day in his fine overstuffed chair and think on what could be, what is, and what might have been, except when his "thinker" became so overwhelmed that he fell soundly to sleep.

The Bible Scholar liked to read and study all day long, for knowledge was the key to his happiness. He studied on this scripture, he studied on that scripture, and he studied about what others thought about this scripture and that. Mostly he delighted on how very much he knew - or thought he knew, anyway.

The Theologian knew all of the religions, great and small. He knew all they agreed on, and all they didn't. He would pace his library floor and ponder all the concepts and dogmas and how they related to mankind. And though he could tell you what each sector believed - he wasn't altogether sure which one was correct; so he pondered some more upon that.

If there was work to be done, Humble Pastor Glen did it, all by himself. He vacuumed the sanctuary floors, and dusted all the pews. He fixed the youth bus, and repaired old leaky faucets. He brightened the church with fresh coats of paint. He even mowed and trimmed the small patch of grass the children loved to play on.

One day, as he was busy at work, Humble Pastor Glen saw a family pass with burdens great and heavy. As he wondered how he could make a difference, a Rhema Word quickened his spirit. Then he ran to find his friends.

"Who will take the fruit of Jesus into the community with me," asked Humble Pastor Glen?

"Not I," said the Philosopher - for he considered the dangers of walking the street and the possible rejection. Besides, he was very tired (and just thinking about it made him fall soundly to sleep).

"Not I," said the Bible Scholar - for he had not completely studied the scriptures on "the fruit being taken into the community" yet. He decided he would pick up a book on that subject and see what others had to say about it.

"Not I," said the Theologian - for he had much too important issues to think about. He thought he might study the major religions and do a survey on what each of them felt about the concept of "fruit in the community." "Hmmm, that would be interesting."

"Then I will reach out myself," said Humble Pastor Glen.

AND HE DID!

When the people received Jesus, Humble Pastor Glen became very excited. "Who will help me care for these new sheep," he asked.

"Not I," said the Philosopher - for he was still trying to figure out what horrible past had put these "sheep" in such turmoil to begin with. He was sure he really didn't want to know, and he didn't want to take a chance that they really weren't changed at all.

"Not I," said the Bible Scholar - for he was still researching the benefits of "reaching out" had not come to an absolute conclusion that there was an unrefuted scripture to support it. Only after coming to the absolute conclusion that "reaching out" was scripturally correct in the mind of every Bible Scholar could he even contemplate studying the scriptural basis of "caring for the sheep."

"Not I," said the Theologian - for he was still on the survey and the percentages were not looking good for the "reaching out" issue. "Perhaps," he thought, "I should begin a new survey which incorporates the 'caring for the sheep' concept. Hmmm, that would be interesting."

"Then I will care for them myself," said Humble Pastor Glen.

AND HE DID!

All summer long, Humble Pastor Glen went into the streets and spoke to the hurting and helpless. He brought them food, taught them about Jesus and showed them someone cared. After weeks and months, one by one, they gave their heart to the Lord. Soon it was time to bring them to his peaceful church.

"Who will drive the bus to pick up the people who want to know more about Jesus," asked Humble Pastor Glen?

"Not I," said the Philosopher. "The nerve," he thought, "to ask such an important person as me to drive a bus!"

"Not I," said the Bible Scholar - but he made a note to be sure and study the scriptures on "bus driving."

"Not I," said the Theologian, and off he went to mail a new survey. "Hmmm, that would be very interesting."

"Then I will drive the bus myself," said Humble Pastor Glen.

AND HE DID!

When the bus route was set and the schedules posted, Humble Pastor Glen set up the programs to tend to the peoples' spiritual needs.

"The people need to be greeted, made to feel welcome, shown around the building and given a bulletin. Who will usher them into God's chambers," asked Humble Pastor Glen?

"Not I," said the Philosopher - for he was still sure they were going to return to their old heathen ways and he didn't want to be around when they did.

"Not I," said the Bible Scholar - for he was just finishing his study on "reaching out," and although it appeared that it was going to be scripturally sound, he still had the "caring for the sheep" issue and the "driving the bus" issue to resolve. He promised to put "ushering in" on his list of studies.

"Not I," said the Theologian - for the survey of the major denominations on "reaching out" was looking quite against the issue, "taking care" was only half complete, but not looking good, and "bus driving" was still in the mail. But, "ushering in," "Hmmm, that would be interesting."

"Then I will usher them in myself," said Humble Pastor Glen.

AND HE DID!

Humble Pastor Glen welcomed every person with a handshake and a smile, passed out the fliers and guided a few tours to the men's and women's "Facilities." He even kissed a few babies and piggy-backed a toddler or two. He introduced the previous members to the new attendees and started them talking about interests in common. Everyone felt very welcome.

After everyone was seated, and quite content, Humble Pastor Glen preached the most humble and satisfying message about "reaching out" and "saving the lost," everybody thought so, even the Philosopher, the Bible Scholar, and the Theologian. All in all, the service was very successful.

The next day Humble Pastor Glen pondered ways to teach his congregation about Jesus and the Biblical ways. Evening Bible Studies and Cell Group Mentoring would greatly add to his humble Sunday services. Humble Pastor Glen called out to his friends, "Who will help me teach the Bible and Mentor the congregation?"

"Not I," said the Philosopher - for that was too below his standing, and besides, wasn't it enough that he was giving up Sunday morning for church. Thinking was hard work, let someone else do it. Besides, he was tired (and just thinking about it made him fall soundly to sleep).

"Not I," said the Bible Scholar - for he was much too busy studying to even consider stopping to teach. And this "Mentoring" business, he was just sure he had never seen the word "Mentor" in the King James Version of the Bible. Let someone else do it.

"Not I," said the Theologian - for every survey he'd completed so far was either against this whole program or had been invalidated because there wasn't anyone else out there who had even considered such a thing, let alone tried it. He surely wasn't going to get mixed up in something that might fail.

"Then I will teach and mentor them myself," said Humble Pastor Glen. AND HE DID!

The church grew and flourished. Many were healed, many delivered. Families were restored and people waxed strong in God's Word. Those that were the fruit of Humble Pastor Glen's seed were raised up to lead, and they did so with a grateful heart, for they remembered from whence they came.

Music filled the sanctuary all week long. People danced, people laughed, people sang, people cried, and people drew together in a new and wonderful family. It was a sweet, sweet fragrance in the nostrils of God.

That fragrance traveled outside of the church, into the city streets, into the homes of the people, and into their workplaces. It was so clear that God had blessed the church and the congregation of Humble Pastor Glen.

When other church leaders would see the miracles there, they would venture the question of how such a miracle could be. "Who was responsible for this fruit enriched land," they would ask.

Humble Pastor Glen would always reply, "Not I." For he knew it was a special gift, sent for the fruit of his labor, direct from the throne room of God.

In Jesus' Name

"That at the name of Jesus every knee should bow, of things in heaven,
and things in earth, and things under the earth;" Philipians 2:10
Life, I claim You,
In Jesus' name,
Beauty pure and free.
Love, I show you,
In Jesus' name,
All the world to see.
Lord, I praise you,
In Jesus' name,
You're everything to me.
Gentle Days and tender nights,
Throughout eternity.
I smile with every sun lit sky,
As gentle breezes blow.
I joy with every star filled sky,
The Heavens all aglow.
I warm with every tender bud,
Drawn open by the rain.
I know they were all given me,
When I called in Jesus' name.
Gentle days and tender nights,
Throughout eternity.

In the Gap

"And he stood between the dead and the living; and the plague was
stayed."
Numbers 16:48

I stand in the summer of my life,
weighing and balancing
yesterday and tomorrow.
I have made a choice,
I have taken my stand
on the firm foundation of truth.
Yesterday's worldly decisions haunt and torment me,
calling out from behind the veil of blood,
that separates me from a deadly past.
The Spirit of God allows me to remember,
Burdening my heart for the souls left behind.
My eyes don't want to see them,
my ears don't want to hear them,
for what they are,
I once was.
But the Spirit calls me to them,
to pray.
I fill my censor with sweet incense,
lighting the fragrance from the fire
of the altar of sacrifice.
I step into the land of giants,
the essence of God in my hand,

the words of God in my mouth.
My soul trembles, my heart breaks,
as I look into the empty, hollow eyes
of the children.
Who will help them to choose?
There to the right is the goodness of God.
There is mercy and grace,
peace and rest.
This is the life I have chosen to share.

There at the left are the quick and simple pleasures,
received at a price,
packaged so elegantly, temptingly, deceivingly.
Snares so easily fallen into.
My prayers cry out,
praying the lost away from temptation.
My testimony gives them hope,
I am proof that there is a way out.
The fragrance of intercession
strengthens the fire in the censor.
The wings of angels gently move the aroma
through the crowd.
For a moment they turn and look.
For a moment they taste the sweetness of the manna
that is laid before them.
For a moment the lure of sin is stopped.
For some it will only take that one moment
to recognize and follow the truth.
For some it may take two or three glimpses
to birth their testimony.
Yet, for others, it may take moment after moment after moment
to break the generational curses

that have trapped them on the path of destruction.
There, in the fields of the land of the giants,
I lay down my life,
as a living sacrifice,
daily standing in the gap,
between the living and the dead.
There will I stand again tomorrow,
my censor lit,
my prayers rising up,
as a sweet sacrifice to heaven.
There, in intercession, will I stand,
turning as many eyes as the Spirit can touch,
to the right.
Believing that every seed planted will root and grow.
Believing in the resurrecting power,
from death to life,
that rests in the anointing.
Believing that the eternal plague can be stayed,
by the strength of my faith.
I cannot stop my sacred vigil,
for the fear rests in my soul,
that in any moment of disconcern,
I might miss one child
that might have looked.

Hold Us Close

"And they said one to another, Did not our heart burn within us, while he talked with us by the way, and while he opened to us the scriptures?" Luke 24:32

We come to you, Oh, Lord,
Our hearts we open wide,
Sweet angels guide us home,
Through prayer we're safe inside.
Keep hunger in our souls,
Sweet fillings every day,
We'll gently teach your Word,
And live you ways.
Please hold us close, Oh, Lord,
The way is dark and steep,
We comfort in Your love,
With joy we weep.
Please walk with us, Oh Lord,
You've sent us to the world;
Their lives are dark and lost,
We're here to stop their hurt.
Put mercy in our souls,
Your perfect love we seek;
For danger stands nearby,
Each time we speak.
We represent Your truths,
Our Joy must never dim;
That all may want to know,
The peace within.

We drink Your word, Oh Lord,
Our hearts and souls are filled.
Your teachings guide our steps,
Our fears and hurts are stilled.
We come in daily prayer,
Our vigils never cease.
We gladly intercede,
To bring our brothers peace.
Please guide each step, Oh Lord,
To keep our witness true,
Your Spirit lights our path,
Each faithful step renews.

Into Every Hand

"If ye then, being evil, know how to give good gifts unto your children,
how much more shall your Father which is in heaven give good things
to them that ask him?"
Matthew 7:11

Into every person's hand,
God brings life.
Sometimes they are the children, of our passion;
Sometimes the children, of our compassion;
Sometimes the hopes and dreams, of our soul.
And with the honor, comes obligation;
to breathe truth, to breathe love,
to breathe hope, to breathe light,
into that life.
With the guard of ministering angels, life can grow.
But tempted by the guard of the fallen,
they find anger, they find strife,
they embrace perversion.
We choose their angels, in their toddler years;
They choose their angels, in their teens;
All choose again, in the maturing of life.
Where have we sent them, these precious lives?
What have we shown them?
What example have we set?
Do the angels of our light,
war with the angels, of their darkness;
Or do the angels of our darkness,
strive to drive away the angels, of their light?

Into every hand, God places the gift of life.
Some are the children, of our passion;
Some are the children, of our compassion;
Some are the hopes and dreams,
of our soul.

Joy

"And now come I to thee; and these things I speak in the world, that they might have my joy fulfilled in themselves." John 17:13

I hold in my hand,
the gift of Joy.
It's my gift,
to do with,
what I will.
I can place it in my pocket,
hide it from the world,
enjoy it only in my private place,
where no one else can see.
Or I can choose to share it,
with a friend,
with a stranger,
with you.
It takes courage to remove it,
from my hand,
and place it,
into my heart,
where it can be criticized,
ridiculed,
shared.
It's my gift,
and it's my choice.
God gave it to me,

to do as I will,
In hopes that I will do,
His will,
and give it,
to you.

Confession

"For thou, Lord, art good, and ready to forgive; and plenteous in mercy unto all them that call upon thee." Psalm 86:5

Forgive me, Lord, for my doubts.
Forgive me, Lord, in my pain and fatigue,
Your voice was distant and faint,
I thought You didn't care.
Forgive me, Lord, I forgot the blessings,
Of yesterday in the crisis,
Of today.
Forgive me, Lord, for not recognizing,
How very precious I am to You,
You showed me again and again,
Buy my self-esteem couldn't receive it.
Thank you, Lord, for continually calling my name,
Calling louder and louder,
When my ears were turned away.
Thank you, Lord, for the friends and warriors,
That You sent to my side,
When I was too weak to fight.
Thank you, Lord, for forced rest,
When my body was in desperate need,
But I refused to rest.
Thank you, Lord, that I am Your daughter,
And You are my Father,
And nothing can ever change that.

Lady In Waiting

"Favour is deceitful, and beauty is vain: but a woman that feareth the
Lord, she shall be praised." Proverbs 31:30

I'm resting, Lord,
here in Your shadow.
Wars wage at my right,
and along my left.
Famine and failure,
Torture,
even the most strong fear,
but I'm safe here,
beneath Your wing.
I know the paths around me,
are tainted with sin,
that dangers lurk,
at every turn,
but I fear not.
You, Lord, have sent angels,
to guide my path,
to set my feet,
one in front of the other,
straight ahead,
not to the right,
not to the left.
I have placed my feet,
in faith,
knowing You have set,
a safe path,

before me.
I have listened carefully,
for Your call,
I have trimmed the wicks,
and replenished the oil,
for the night watch.
For the time when,
My Beloved may call.
I practice my stitching,
in purple and red,
as I wait.
Keeping my mind flooded,
with the constant blessing,
my Lord has bestowed,
upon me.
Delicate, sure, stitches,
adorn the robe,
my Lord will wear,
when the day is come.
Each placed with a prayer,
each outlining a blessing,
each anointed,
with the tongues of angels.
I wait at Your feet,
precious one,
as the night passes once again.
Catching a glimpse of You,
a glancing touch,
bringing such peace,
strengthening my desire.
I wait, with the gifts of my hand,
gifts of my heart,

gifts of my tongue.
I wait, for the day You will call,
and draw me to Your chamber,
to share in the riches,
kept deep inside.
The wait seems long,
but holds no burden,
only the treasure,
of promises seen,
and promises known,
and truths only realized,
by lovers.
I wait for the day,
You will come to my chamber,
and raise my hand,
to a delicate kiss.
There will we dance,
for the joy,
and the treasure,
held in intimate bonds,
of true love.
Until that day,
My Beloved,
My Lord,
I will wait,
and prepare,
and rest,
that I might not miss,
one moment with You.

Fresh Beginnings

"A Song of degrees. I will lift up mine eyes unto the hills, from whence cometh my help. My help cometh from the Lord, which made heaven and earth." Psalm 121:1-2

I love my morning cup of coffee. Nothing fluffy or sweet or blended, just fresh ground, brewed coffee. I claimed it as my last vice, until recently that is.

Having food allergies, all of my fun food was disappearing - one item at a time (bummer). People were always curious at my unusual diet and would inquire at my ability to stick with it. "It's easy," I'd reply, "I still have my morning coffee to look forward to."

Well! Pride goes before the fall and it wasn't too long after that the doctor removed my coffee. I pled, rationalized and begged - to no avail. Coffee was out!

I went before the Lord and "Pitched a Fit." I'm so grateful that my Jesus is patient and understanding of me. "What is it that you so enjoy about your cup of coffee," He asked me.

"The aroma," I said. "The feel of the warm cup nestled between my hands. The minutes I get to blow a cooling breath across the top while sipping the robust drink. The moments I get alone, enjoying the morning and reflecting on the goodness of God."

A smile touched my lips and my sorrow faded. It wasn't the cup of coffee I missed - it was the fellowship and tender times with God that I was afraid of losing. The aroma of a fresh morning, the grass wet with dew. The warmth inside that He spreads, from the top of my head to the bottom of my feet. The cooling breath of God as a breeze caresses my cheek. Sipping of His goodness - if only for a few minutes before my day begins.

Lord, let me never lose touch with what the true meaning is, of everything I do. Let me release the ritual and enter directly into your presence - with praise and thanksgiving and joy.

The Mantle

And these are the garments which they shall make; a breastplate, and
an ephod, and a robe, and a broidered coat, a mitre, and a girdle: and
they shall make holy garments for Aaron thy brother, and his sons,
that he may minister unto me in the priest's office. Exodus 28:4

The angels descend
from Heavenly shields
and Whisper – beckon
calling my name.
"Rise, child,
the time has come
to walk from under
the covering of another
and buckle on
the Mantle of God."
The Words of God,
etched in my heart,
and the joy of Thanksgiving
give me the strength
to carry the 12 precious stones
into the holy of holies.
The light from the Golden Candle Stick,
with 7 brilliant flames,
fed with the most pure oil,
pressed forth by the prayers
of the saints,

glisten through the stones,
reflecting the rainbow of promise,
on the fine white linen
that lines the chamber of the temple
that dwells within my Spirit.
"Pray, child, pray,"
they gently whisper,
"for today the Ark will be lifted,
from its place of rest,
onto the shoulders,
of the Priests."
"Not one foot must stumble,
not one pole can fall,
for the poles that carry the Ark
must remain high.
This Ark,
Which houses the very stones,
etched by the finger of God,
must not touch the tainted soil
marred by the pride of man."
"Hold up the priests,
strengthen their backs,
purify their path
with tears and prayer.
Nurture their spirit
with your trust
and encouragement."
"Buckle on the mantle, child,
for the kingdom depends
on the courage of the Saints."
Now I stand,
ready to receive,

ready to protect,
the most precious gift,
my heritage,
which stems from one
of those twelve
precious stones.

The Mustard Seed

"If ye have faith as a grain of mustard seed, ye shall say unto this mountain, Remove hence to yonder place; and it shall remove; and nothing shall be impossible unto you." Matthew 17:20

While enjoying a moment of prayer and being enveloped in the blessing of anointed music, I was touched by the greatness of God. The God that brought the children of promise out of Egypt; the God that parted the Red Sea; the God that brought life to the womb of a virgin Israelite girl; the God who created life and set the sun, moon and stars in their orbit. The God that give life to the grass, flowers, animals and man – no two alike. The God that holds every thought and every emotion of each of His children close to His heart, and turns His head toward the broken, sincere prayer.

What a Mighty God We Serve!!!

As I sat in thanksgiving of how great He is, I rejoiced in how He loves us so much that He has packaged all of His power into a faith that would fit inside the tiny mustard seed. A seed so small, that I could hold hundreds in the palm of my hand.

That thought fills me with such joy. The faith of Moses, Elijah, Elisha, Peter and Paul would fit into five tiny seeds that rest in the crease of my palm. The faith to lead a nation, to speak life into dying people. The faith to perplex natural events and raise the dead back to new life. The faith to stand, and when they were weary and no longer had the strength to stand, by faith they stood.

Jesus, I pray that I will be content enough with myself that I will want to abundantly bless another in my smallness. I don't want to feel that I must be well known and in frontline ministry to be able to make a difference. Help me to remember that I can rest in prayer, and with the faith the size of a mustard seed, send up the sweet savor of a miracle to be birthed in another, half a world away.

For Granted

"The Lord liveth; and blessed be my rock; and let the God of my
salvation be exalted." Psalm 18:46

Have I taken you for granted, Lord?
Can You forgive me?
Do you understand the pain of Circumstance,
That clouds reason.
You patiently wait as I blame you,
For events You had nothing to do with.
You sing to me songs of Love,
When I feel the depths of worthlessness.
You send me tender arms,
When I feel unloved and unlovable.
You send me songs of joy,
When tears steal my night.
You wake me with a tender caress,
Inviting me to intimate times with You.
You speak into my life the words of strength,
Courage and wisdom,
As I open the pages of Your Word.
You fill my mouth with the tongues of Angels,
A private language that only we understand.
Lord, do I take you for granted?
Will you forgive me.

New Wineskins

Neither do men put new wine into old bottles: else the bottles break, and the wine runneth out, and the bottles perish: but they put new wine into new bottles, and both are preserved. Matthew 9:17

The old wineskin,
that covers this frame,
has become stiff,
and tough,
and bitter.
The New Wine,
that once filled this frame,
has been tasted,
and rejected,
and spit upon the ground,
leaving an empty skin,
tainted with yesterday's desires,
allowed to go stale.
Like an old wineskin,
in the skillful hands,
of the Master,
it is time to have the stiffness,
beaten down,
the bitterness boiled out,
and the callousness,
scrapped away.
Cleansed,

supple, resilient,
once again this frame,
will be prepared to carry within,
the New Wine,
daily fresh,
daily blessed.
This time, Lord,
let me not sniff at,
let me not swirl around,
let me not fretfully sip,
and let me not spit out,
the New Wine,
placed inside.
But, let me savor,
every drop,
no matter the flavor,
or what I wish it might be,
or what I wish it could have been.
Let me cherish,
the new wine,
I've been prepared,
to carry,
that I've been sent,
to pour out.
And once again,
when I've allowed the wine,
to grow bitter and taint,
renew the wineskin,
that covers this frame,
making it better,
than the first day,
it was sent,

to be a vessel,
destined to hold the best wine,
the wine that is served,
at the throne of the King.

Cycle

"And he said, My presence shall go with thee, and I will give thee rest."
Exodus 33:14

The rose bushes are pruned and bare, dormant.
The valleys are brown, dry.
The air is crisp, clean, clear.
Crystals of cold hang in the air, waiting.
From the first appearance,
It seems as though death has come to overcome.
Look closer still.
The cold releases dew, seeping deep underground.
The brief glimpses of sunlight beacon tender buds,
Soon the cycle of life resumes.
Like seasoned Christians;
Pruned, trimmed, resting.
The Love of God surges forth,
When weariness gives way to rest in the Son.

Only By Faith

And he said to the woman, Thy faith hath saved thee; go in peace.
Luke 7:50

By faith stood Abraham,
in the promise of Isaac.
By grace it came to pass.
overcoming natural life,
birthing a child,
in a lonely golden year.
Faith took the promise,
and blew life into lifelessness.
Faith saw Isaac as the sown seed,
laughter come at last,
then grace matured it,
multiplying it.
Fourteen generations flowed,
from Abraham to David,
through Jacob and Obed,
and Jesse.
Fourteen generations flowed from David,
until the carrying away into Babylon,
through Solomon,
through Manasses,
through Josias.
Then fourteen more flowed,
from Babylon to Christ,
the Word manifest in flesh,
the Keeper of eternity.

through Achim,
Eleazar to Jacob,
the father of Joseph,
the husband of Mary,
the mother of Christ.
By faith did Mary accept the promise,
that grew within her womb.
By faith did Joseph accept Mary,
heavy with child,
not of his loins, not of his love.
By grace they stood as one,
on a destined night,
the sky brightened,
by the Glory of God,
in the shape of a star,
pointing down to the Son.
By faith Joseph took Jesus,
adopted now, into the lineage of Abraham,
adopted now, as a child of promise.
By grace Joseph watched,
as He grew to a man,
well before His years.
Our perfect pattern,
our Shepherd and King.
Now, by faith, we trust in His Word,
our heritage blessed by driven saints,
and tarnished by those who did evil,
in the sight of the Lord.
By faith are we accepted,
are we adopted into His kingdom,
joint-heirs with Christ,
children of promise,

just as He did so long ago.
By grace will we walk,
in His footsteps,
as best as we are able,
crying out for strength,
for peace, for love.
By faith we receive all,
grace has promised, and more,
for only by our limited faith,
can we see into,
God's limitless plan.

A Pebble In My Shoe

"Who can say, I have made my heart clean, I am pure from my sin?"
Proverbs 20:9

There's a pebble in my shoe,
One of those small odd shaped ones,
That often fall securely to the side,
Only rubbing a little.
Not a big pebble,
Yet not too small.
I know it's there,
I know it doesn't belong,
But it isn't so large that I need to stop,
To empty it out.
In fact, if I toss my foot just so,
I hardly know it's there.
Once in a while,
It jumps right out of its crease,
And settles beneath my heel,
Zapping me back to the realization,
That it really doesn't belong.
Then I shake my foot again,
And send it off,
To hide in a crease.
I could shake it out,
But I've grown accustomed to its presence,
It's sort of a game,
How far can I walk without getting zapped.
And it's like having a deep secret,

That no one else knows.
Sometimes I talk to it,
It's like an old friend,
Then it bruises a toe,
And becomes an agitation.
Soon I'll toss it out,
I can do it any time I want.
I think.
It won't matter if I toss it out,
Or if it stays,
It doesn't affect me that much,
At least not than anyone else would notice.
Well, except for those who see me limp,
Or occasionally jump.
But otherwise, no one can tell.
I have a pebble in my shoe,
I call it sin.

Out of the Mouth of Babes

Out of the mouth of babes and sucklings hast thou ordained strength because of thine enemies, that thou mightest still the enemy and the avenger. Psalm 8:2

The other day I took my 6-year-old son to the mall for "one-on-one" Mom-Son time. We saw a short 3-D movie, "T-REX", the one where the dinosaur drools right in your lap as he eyes you for a potential lunch item. After the movie we ate lunch (30 restaurants to choose from and he goes for Burger King - AGAIN!) and talked a while, then we decided to do a sightseeing lap around the mall.

About 2 months ago I started working Saturday mornings, the day I usually spend with the boys. We always went for breakfast (all you could eat buffets!) and then went to the park or ran errands around the valley. When my schedule changed I went to the boy's school and asked the principal about taking each boy out on rotating Fridays. She gave me her approval as well as her blessing; Mom-Son Friday came to pass. Every Friday at noon I pick one of the boys up. We talk, eat and watch a movie (of the boy's choice); not necessarily in that order. By 4:00 PM we're on the way back to pick-up the other two and head home. This particular day was Jon's day.

As Jon and I walked around he chose the shops he wanted to tour through. Being 6 he chose only the brightest and most colorful shops. No clothing - mostly shops with toys, hanging objects, shelf decorations and rocks. One of the shops we went into seemed innocent from the front. There were rock slab wind-chimes, polished stone necklaces, cut stone book-ends, and similar items throughout. Jon was mesmerized by the color and shine.

As we neared the back of the store we saw voodoo and witch-doctor paraphernalia on the floor and walls. I tried to steer Jon clear of the items, but he nearly ran into a chair with a demon head carved into the seat back.

Jon stopped immediately, put his little fists on his hips (as only a 6-year-old can do) and stated quite clearly, "Well, these people don't know Jesus." After which he quickly dismissed himself from the store.

Trying to help lift his spirits, I started searching for signs of Jesus in every store we entered. Finally, as we reached the end of the mall, I spotted a shelf with porcelain figurines of Jesus, Mary, the nativity, the crucifix and various other Christian themes.

"There, Jon," I said. "There's Jesus."

For a moment a smile formed on his face, which was quickly dismissed and replaced by round determined eyes and firmly set fists.

"Well," he said. "I just want to know why Jesus is there - and women with no clothes are right there!" I followed his small pointing finger to the shelf immediately below. There on the shelf were porcelain nudes, three times the size of the Christian figurines.

"I'm just going to go get Joseph (our youth pastor) and we're going to come back here and pray." At that point he took is offended little self out of the store and decided that he had seen enough of the mall.

So there I was, at 49, looking so hard to find Jesus that I allowed myself to overlook the offense, the insult, of placing Him among the very decadence He came to this world to overcome. In that very store were dragons and Buddas, crystals and prayer beads, nudes and seductive paintings. How many times do I close my eyes to the things that offend me? How many times have I felt it was the way of the world and there was nothing I could do?

Out of the mouth of a babe came the words that had been spoken into him. At 6 years old he was ready to take a stand against the things he knew were wrong, and he was ready to find someone to stand with him in prayer.

Thank you, Jesus, for babies who remind us how to be the best we can be.

God of Our Fathers

"But with the precious blood of Christ, as of a lamb without blemish
and without spot:"
1 Peter 1:19

God of our fathers,
Perfect and true,
Tender Your Children,
Cleanse us anew.
Merciful Savoir,
Source of new life,
God of our fathers,
Our precious delight.

The Phenomena of the

America "Christian"

"But ye believe not, because ye are not of my sheep, as I said unto you. My sheep hear my voice, and I know them, and they follow me: And I give unto them eternal life; and they shall never perish, neither shall any man pluck them out of my hand. [29] My Father, which gave them me, is greater than all; and no man is able to pluck them out of my Father's hand. [30] I and my Father are one." John 10:26-30

My husband and I made the decision to become foster parents. After a year of classes and paperwork, we were blessed with two little boys, which we were allowed to adopt four years later. To say we have been blessed by our decision is an understatement, although it has not always been easy.

When we brought these boys into our lives, we were extremely involved in church, choir, teaching, Bible study, helps and various other church activities. The boys were thrust into a culture they never knew existed. Being church "staff kids" meant they often spend 10 to 12 hours a day at the church in different aspects of school and ministry. They received a "crash coarse" in Christianity and were excited to share this delight with the world.

It was not uncommon for them to stop perfect strangers and ask questions or give lectures of the values of "keeping the temple clean" (no smoking, drinking or drugs) (1 Corinthians 6:19-20). Being lectured by a 3-year-old or a 5-year-old on what harm certain substances can do to your body can be amusing, irritating, condemning or all three.

Going to the grocery store or drug store was always an adventure. Restaurants were unpredictable - they knew they had a captive audience; the waiter or waitress.

We never knew when or what they were going to say. They held a boldness I never had when it came to their faith. The amazing thing is, that with their wide-eyed innocence, people always answered. That is what this is all about. Not about the innocent questioning, it's about the answers.

I had read that Americans consider themselves to be Christians, simply because they are Americans! Several people responded in just that manner - "sure, I'm a Christian - I'm an American!" but, when pinned down about which church they attended - they didn't. When they did, it was for Christmas, Easter and Weddings.

One young man said that he wasn't a Christian, his mom was. He said he was a Christian once, but he quit going to church. He knew he needed to start going back, but he was busy. Sunday was his sleep-in day.

One young man said he wasn't a Christian, he was a Baptist! And several LDS said they were Christians, even though they don't believe Jesus is the son of God.

We met several people who were obviously into New Age, but believed they were Christians. We even knew of people who claimed to be "white witches" who felt they were Christians. People who attend church on Sunday and read horoscopes every day of the week. People who pray at bedtime and call psychics during the day. It's the phenomena of the American "Christian."

I, myself, spent several years in a denominational church and was never encouraged to read the Bible (2 Timothy 2:15), never told that horoscopes were forbidden (Isaiah 47:13-14), or that psychics were cursed (Leviticus 20:21). I didn't know "white" witchcraft was "witchcraft" trying to make itself look "good" instead of "evil" (Deuteronomy 18:10-12). I have prayed many, many hours over this phenomena. What is the answer?

The word of the Lord came to me "Then saith he unto his disciples, The harvest truly is plenteous, but the labourers are few; [38] Pray ye therefore the Lord of the harvest, that he will send forth labourers into his harvest" (Matthew 9:37-38). The mission field begins in our own home. The mission field is at our front door.

Because America does not have to fight to have freedom of religion, the people don't understand what true Christianity is. In those countries where they lay down their lives for an hour a week to gather together in prayer and Bible study - you can believe they understand. We dwell in a country where we know a little bit about everything - but very few know a lot about any one particular thing; especially, it seems, pure Christianity.

We, the Church, have allowed confusion, distraction, and laziness to enter into the message we were sent to share (Galatians 1:6-8). It crept in, ever so quietly, and took its place among the once dedicated. Now we are sent to search it out.

There in the curiosity of my two children dwelt an answer. Where I had been content for someone to verify they were a Christian, now I knew the mission was to make sure that they knew what Christianity was and how to come to the saving grace of Christ. It is each of our jobs to steer the confused from horoscopes to scriptures - from psychics to Jesus.

Jesus, let me always be mindful of the enemy we battle and the subtle ways he perverts the truth. Let me not be pacified with quick answers that may leave a soul, believing they are walking righteously, in the hands of an evil curse. Let me speak up, at my own discomfort, to bring that little lost sheep back home.

Lord of the Dance

"A time to weep, and a time to laugh; a time to mourn, and a time to dance;" Ecclesiastics. 3:4

Take My hand as I draw you near,
Rest your cheek tenderly against Mine.
My arm holds firmly across your back,
You are fully enveloped in My love.
This is our time of intimacy.
Now step boldly back, secure in My love, safe.
Dance before Me, as a delicate flower.
The sweet fragrance so intoxicating.
This is our time of thankfulness.
Step back again and dance fervently,
Firmly plant your feet,
Chase away the evil with your hands.
Fight away the temptation that searches out our children.
This is our time of intercession.
As you grow faint, weary in the battle,
Step back to me, safely in My arms, enveloped in My arms,
Receiving My strength, receiving My love,
This is our time of renewing.
Take My hand.

Running Away

"Train up a child in the way he should go: and when he is old, he will not depart from it." Proverbs 22:6

I have been most blessed. God has given me three wonderful boys to love, encourage, and enjoy. Each of them has a strong call of God upon their lives, all in different capacities. We call each one by the name God has placed upon our heart – Pastor Jon, Deacon Eli and Chaplain Paul. In the body of Christ, all positions are of equal importance (1 Cor 12:12), this we have shown them so that neither feels of less importance than the other.

Having children called to the ministry is a tremendous challenge. The challenge isn't in Bible study or scripture memorization, they strive to meet those desires themselves. The challenge is in recognizing the Spiritual Warfare and the schemes of the enemy that tempt them away from the call God has upon them.

Although there are many stories of miracles and answered prayer for each of them, our greatest challenge has been with our oldest, Paul. Paul is a teenager, raised most of his life in Christian education, but placed into the public school system during the 8th grade, when the Christian school he had been attending closed. Placed in an environment he had never been subjected to, the enemy tempted and attacked, stole and taunted. However difficult these trials were, they couldn't compare to the luring and wooing that called his name.

With peer pressure and Satan's enticing whispers, Paul was drawn into a life we never expected. Although the rejection of family values was difficult for us, it was the running away that tormented our family. Where was he? Was he eating? Did he have a safe place to sleep? Who is he with? Why has he left us? Doesn't he love us anymore?

Doesn't he love us anymore. Rejection by your own child. Harsh words and accusations fly about. Why didn't we see this coming. Only prayer brings us peace, difficult travailing prayer. I can't begin to explain the depth of emotions a parent goes through in circumstances such as these. Love, hope, anger, hopelessness. Faith, doubt, pain, faith. Sorrow, prayer, memories, trust.

As I prayed one night, I asked God if He could understand the special relationship that grows as you hold that baby, child, young man in your arms and protect him from every possible danger that could come against him - God showed me Jesus, sent to earth to be born in a lowly manger, vulnerable to man, protected by the angels; the same angels that he has sent to watch over my son. I asked God if He could ever understand the pain and the rejection of a child not wanting to be near you, after you've been his best friend for most of his life - God showed me Jesus, standing before the crowd, as they chose Barabas to live and Jesus to die. I asked God if He knew what it felt like to sit in your child's room, empty, hollow, except for the memories that line the walls and shelves - God showed me Golgotha, and Jesus' lifeless body on the cross. I asked God if He could understand the pain of searching every street, every car, looking closely at every child the same age and build, in hopes of seeing your child, even at a distance - God showed me the people at the cross, dividing Jesus' clothes, cutting into His lifeless body with a spear, laughing at all He was, void of any righteousness or desire of God. I asked God if He knew what it was like, waiting for the phone to ring or the front door to open, just to hear your child's voice calling again, waiting , praying - God opened my ears to hear Jesus' last cry, "Why hast thou forsaken me?"

Yes, He knows. He gave His son willingly, to walk in places of evil that all may be saved, even my son. He gave His son to bring hope, life and peace, knowing the pain and agony His son had to feel before it could be done. He watched as everything His son did was rejected and scorned, even as He lay lifeless. Yes, He knows.

Then God reminded me of the many times I have turned from Him. How many times have I turned my back on the family He has placed me in? How many times have I rejected the values and desires He has placed inside me? How many times have I spoken harsh and hurting words to Him, as I ran away to a world of selfish pleasure? How many times have I simply chosen to be somewhere else instead of in the sweet relationship with my Father? How many times have I put other things, people, places before Him? How many others have done the same? Forgive us Lord, with your unlimited mercy, for all the times we fell to temptation and disappointed You. Forgive me, Lord, for thinking that You could never understand the pain of a Mother. Remind me that you are in control of all things. Help me to trust You and run back to You all of my days.

Little Bit More

"The law of the Lord is perfect, converting the soul: the testimony of
the Lord is sure, making wise the simple." Psalm 19:7

Lord, in my temptations you hold me,
Through sorrows and tears You are there.
When all of the world is against me,
I truthfully know that You care.
As each day unfolds I find trials,
And burdens too heavy to bare.
I humbly come in Your presence,
And lay them before You in prayer.
I'm nothing without You beside me,
You teach me Your words that I share.
When falling, I pray that You'll guide me,
And I'll shine just a little bit more.
Lord, each day you give life new meaning,
My old life's a memory gone past;
My worldly possessions lose value,
Your love is all that will last.
You touch me each morning with fire,
And rivers of water run through;
I can't even think of tomorrow,
Without knowing that I have You.
You've lifted me out of dark shadows,
And endless confusion and strife;
Your mercy and grace has renewed me,

And shown me the beauty of life.
Lord, now has come my time to witness,
And share the beauty I've found;
It's happiness, free for the asking,
Where joy and blessings abound.
I'll teach with honest persuasion,
Myself, an example of praise;
Teaching Your word and Your promise,
Your miracles, works and sound faith.
I'll conquer if You stand beside me,
No enemy dares to cause harm;
Your children will follow in victory,
Wrapped in Your arms safe and warm.

Sacrifice

By him therefore let us offer the sacrifice of praise to God continually, that is, the fruit of our lips giving thanks to his name. Hebrews 13:15

The Ancient of Days,
cast Himself to the earth,
in the form of a seed,
in the womb of a virgin.
Subject, now, to heat and cold,
to fatigue and illness,
to prejudice and ridicule,
to suffering and pain.
The Ancient of Days,
became man,
flesh, blood and Spirit;
willingly giving,
the power of deity,
for the birth of a nation.
The God of Jessie,
born through the sacrifice of blood,
to become the blood sacrifice.
From the promises to Adam,
to the revelation shown John,
the blood of God coursed the earth,
changing strength and direction,
at the tributary called Christ.
The new stream of Christ,

fed the trees of new life,
where the roots of the old,
were washed clean.
The water, most pure,
chased the stagnant pools of red,
that once rinsed man's hands,
but touched not the soul.
The water, most pure,
flowed over and cleansed,
the wounds of the past,
refreshing the hope,
of a dark, tarnished dream.
The water of life,
borne from the blood,
of an innocent man,
takes sweet revenge,
on the deepest of sin.
Released to be washed,
by the power of mercy,
by the treasure of grace,
it rises back up,
to the base of the cross.
There, at the cross,
the blood and water,
of grace and mercy,
flows down to the earth,
as forgiven sin reaches up,
meeting at the feet of Christ.
Running together they became one,
the earth shook with promise,
the sky darkened,
to reveal a new light,

and the rivers flowed,
with a new wine,
washing clean the weary souls,
of all that would reach forth,
in praise.

Kneel With Us

"O come, let us worship and bow down: let us kneel before the Lord our maker."
Psalm 95:6

As we come to You,
We seek the truth,
Our open hearts we give.
We lift our hands,
And take a stand,
in righteousness to live.
Help us speak for You,
In all we do,
Your words of peace we share.
Please hold us near,
And calm our fears,
And kneel with us in prayer.
Lord, we teach Your word,
Your truths are heard,
We walk in love and faith.
We share Your ways,
For strength we pray,
We've learned to kneel and wait.
Keep us in Your will,
Our own thoughts stilled,
Our old ways changed to new.
Please keep us close,

At any cost,
Our mind on only You.
Lord, we lift our hands,
In love we stand,
A shout of faith we raise.
We reach to You,
Your touch renews,
Our words are songs of praise.

Seeking to be filled,
To know Your will,
Fills every waking hour.
Please touch our souls,
And let us know,
Your mercy, strength and power.

Secret Place

"He that dwelleth in the secret place of the most High shall abide under the shadow of the Almighty. I will say of the Lord, He is my refuge and my fortress: my God; in him will I trust." Psalm 91:1-2

I have a secret place,
That I alone know.
A place I call my own,
Where my Father and I,
Laugh together,
And cry together,
Face to face.
It's a very special place,
I can travel to at will,
Without ever leaving,
The place where I stand.
In that secret place,
I see the face of God.
Sometimes in a stranger,
Sometimes in the sky,
As I bask in His Holy Creation.
My secret place has flowers,
And birds,
And streams,
And fields,
Sweet fragrances of memories,
And music that fills my soul,

Things that bring me closer,
To my Father's voice.
You may sit right near me,
And never see me leave,
But you'll notice a different glow,
That saturates my spirit,
And lifts me ever upward.
My secret place can't be found,
By anybody else.
But your's, my friend,
Waits for you,
Deep within your heart.

Thank God

"Surely the righteous shall give thanks unto thy name: the upright
shall dwell in thy presence." Psalm 140:13

In the sunrise, in the clouds above,
In the gentle lifting movement of a dove.
In the quiet of a sweet sleeping child,
Thank God, Thank God.
In the Stillness of a star filled sky,
In the company of loved ones on a cold night.
In the riches and the fullness of life,
Thank God, Thank God.
Thank God,
For the blessings brought before us every day.
For the wonders and the peace in our hearts,
Thank God, Thank God.
For the Spirit, in the hungry soul,
For the Words of truth that teach us of His love.
In the fire, when the pulpit explodes.
Thank God, Thank God.
In the filling of a new born child,
In the words and tongues of Angels spoken prayerfully,
For the moments when He calls out your name,
Thank God, Thank God.
Thank God,
For the blessings brought before us every day.
For the wonders and the peace in our hearts,

Thank God.

Spirit of Man

"The spirit of man is the candle of the Lord, searching all the inward parts of the belly." Proverbs 20:27

Lord, can you see
the death within
the fallen man?
Has the light,
You've placed,
inside his soul,
dimmed from the absence,
of the anointing oil?
Does his inward parts,
grow dark and empty,
from the absence of you?
Where did the oil go?
Did it slowly burn away,
when used on goodly projects,
void of Godly seed?
Did it burn rapidly away,
on endless nights,
of busy details,
none birthed for the kingdom,
only for the furtherance,
of man?
Did the glow leave,
so slowly,
that no one noticed,
the warmth in the depths of the eyes,

was replaced by cold,
hallow, loneliness?
Once cold,
did the soul embrace the emptiness,
and call it home;
explaining the way back,
is too difficult?

Is there yet a hope,
a small smoldering bud,
that a new flame,
could grow,
even brighter,
than the first?
Replenish the oil,
in this vessel, Lord,
that when the nights grow so weary,
I will draw closer to the flame,
and into Your light.
Let there be such an abundance,
that the light within me,
will show into the eyes,
of one so cold.
Let the oil flow,
so heavily,
from my anointing,
that it will flow from my prayers,
through the depths of Jesus,
and into another's life.
Let me always be a light,
to lift the darkness,
in another's soul.

A Brand New Day

"For now we see through a glass, darkly; but then face to face: now I know in part; but then shall I know even as also I am known." 1 Corinthians 13:12

Steam from the frigid water,
Rises up to kiss the sun.
Birds shake loose the morning dew,
And sing the sweetest song.
The leaves and petals raise their face,
To drink the first rays of day.
Music fills the air, chasing away the cold darkness,
Of the night.
Clouds part, allowing the gold and purple hues,
To dance across the sky.
Webs glisten in intricate geometric patterns.
Tiny footprints grace the fresh morning soil.
It's a brand new day and God has given His first gift.
Lord, teach me to see with spiritual eyes,
The same daily beauty I see in the natural.
Remove the scales of circumstance,
That cloud my spiritual vision.
Help me to receive Your morning kiss,
With more joy and admiration,
Than simple nature.
Help me to receive the miracle of NOW.

Stepping Forward

The waters saw thee, O God, the waters saw thee; they were afraid: the depths also were troubled. The clouds poured out water: the skies sent out a sound: thine arrows also went abroad. The voice of thy thunder was in the heaven: the lightnings lightened the world: the earth trembled and shook. Thy way is in the sea, and thy path in the great waters, and thy footsteps are not known. Thou leddest thy people like a flock by the hand of Moses and Aaron. Psalm 77:16-20

Art thou not it which hath dried the sea, the waters of the great deep; that hath made the depths of the sea a way for the ransomed to pass over? Isaiah 51:10

I stand in the path of troubled waters,
urged by a deep stirring in my soul.
My promise awaits me on the other side,
distant, dangerous, seemingly unattainable.
The waters are rising and churning,
lapping the ground at my feet,
teasing, testing, tantalizing.
Dare I step into troubled water,
tempting Satan, testing God?
Is the vision but a dream
or God's perfect will?
There is no Moses to lead me in,
no Aaron to encourage me forth.
The angels hide, wait, watch.
Dare I take a chance

and step into the churning depths?
Do I trust God to part the sea,
dry the ground my feet must travel upon,
and hide my footsteps beneath the returning waters?
Or do I remain in my sheltered life,
no risks taken, nothing lost, nothing gained.
Do I reach out to the will of God,
the high calling I have been predestined to take,
or rest behind,
allowing another to receive the rich blessing
and sense of victory.
The sea of troubled water is frightening,
yet enchanting.
There is so much to gain,
so little to lose.
The waters surge and ebb,
surge and ebb.
Call me forward, Father,
as I strive to please you.
I close my eyes to self,
to doubt, to acceptable mediocrity.
One step at a time I move forward,
one step at a time.
As the waters part and rise up around me
I see the truth of my adversary,
like a motion picture through a looking glass,
larger than life, magnified,
yet fragile and easily destroyed.
Why did I fear?
Will those troubles disappear?
No!
They will always rest in the troubled waters.

It is my choice to view them,
or place my eyes on God,
and take a step forward,
knowing that each step will part the waters
and find solid ground.

Daughter of Zion

"And thou, O tower of the flock, the strong hold of the daughter of Zion, unto thee shall it come, even the first dominion; the kingdom shall come to the daughter of Jerusalem. Now why dost thou cry out aloud? is there no king in thee? is thy counsellor perished? for pangs have taken thee as a woman in travail. Be in pain, and labour to bring forth, O daughter of Zion, like a woman in travail: for now shalt thou go forth out of the city, and thou shalt dwell in the field, and thou shalt go even to Babylon; there shalt thou be delivered; there the Lord shall redeem thee from the hand of thine enemies. Arise and thresh, O daughter of Zion: for I will make thine horn iron, and I will make thy hoofs brass: and thou shalt beat in pieces many people: and I will consecrate their gain unto the Lord, and their substance unto the Lord of the whole earth." Micah 4:8-10

Why do you weep,
Daughter of Zion?
Have you forgotten who you are?
At the hem of your garment,
Cling the children of Israel,
Dare they see your tears?
Why do you cry out,
Daughter of Zion?
Your voice was created,
To put your enemy,
In his place,
Beneath your feet,

Far from the children,
You protect.
Let your tears be saved,
For intercession,
And your crying out,
To birth a new mission,
That your children,
Will take forth.
Forget not that you are birthed,
Of royalty.
A king and a priest.
Stand your station,
And raise your head high.

Forget not that you were birthed,
To counsel.
Prepared to call forth,
The promises and armies,
Of God.
Reclaim the territory,
Stolen by the enemy,
The cities and the lands,
That once were a testimony,
To the One true God.
Stand in faith,
And watch the evil,
Slither away,
As the hand of the Lord,
Forbids its sting.
Stand up,
Daughter of Zion,
With dignity

And righteous pride,
For what is yours.
Don't let the momentary pain,
The enemy has wrought,
Overcome the truth,
Of who you are.
Stand up,
Daughter of Zion.
For into your hand,
Have I placed the hope,
Of the Nations.
Stand Up!

Stones of Fire

"Thou art the anointed cherub that covereth; and I have set thee so: thou wast upon the holy mountain of God; thou hast walked up and down in the midst of the stones of fire." Ezekiel 28:14
"By the multitude of thy merchandise they have filled the midst of thee with violence, and thou hast sinned: therefore I will cast thee as profane out of the mountain of God: and I will destroy thee, O covering cherub, from the midst of the stones of fire." Ezekiel 28:16

When I heard of the Stones of Fire I prayed, "Lord, what are they?"
He said, "They are the tears of God."
"I don't understand," I said, "teach me, Lord."

Stones of fire,
colors so vibrant,
the intensity of God's Spirit,
fighting to escape the stone's housing,
yet trapped there,
to please the eye,
of all who gaze.

He placed His throne,
and rested his feet,
upon brilliant Sapphire,
purged with fire and time,
blue as the deepest sea,
vast as the clearest sky;

this was the third Heaven.

As a lover gives his beloved,
or a father gives his child,
a most precious gift,
God gave His treasure,
a city built upon,
the stones of fire.

In His richness He gave all beauty,
to make a sacred court.
The foundations of the city,
were of the purest stone,
of Jasper, Sapphire and Chalcedony,
Emerald, Sardonyx and Sardius,
Chrysolite, Beryl and Topaz,
Chrysoprasus, Jacinth and Amethyst.
Twelve foundations,
for twelve children to come,
soon to be nations,
then kings and priests.

Children to be raised,
in a perfect Eden,
guarded by angels,
perfection at every glance,
ruler of all they could see.

Yet, in the third Heaven,
where archangels commune with God,
and gold paves the streets,
as pure as crystal glass,

a cry was heard,
as God shed a tear.

The third Heaven wasn't enough,
for Lucifer.

He was the most perfect creation,
to ever walk in the Heavens of God.
He was the most beautiful of all angels,
adorned in the precious stones,
that Heaven was founded on.

His voice sang the arias,
as an orchestra,
he was the most anointed,
the most wise,
until his beauty,
beguiled his own heart,
and iniquity became his god.
Refusing to serve,
demanding the highest kingdom,
Lucifer fell,
cast from the splendor of Heaven,
pulled down by the weight,
cursed with the fire,
that charged the beauty,
of the precious stones,
he proudly wore.

Down in a wilderness,
walked 12 nations,
trying to purge their lives,

of desire and deceit.

Set over an Ephod,
Secured to the Breastplate,
carried on the shoulders,
of the High Priest,
were 12 stones.
Each stone for a nation,
in four rows of three,
according to their birth.

On the top was the Sardius, Topaz and Carbuncle,
then was the Emerald, Sapphire and Diamond,
next was the Ligure, Agate and Amethyst,
last was the Beryl, Onyx and Jasper,
held at the top and the sides,
by pure gold.
Once again God's pride,
was adorned by His precious gift.

All seemed well until the days,
man's faith-filled leader,
took time with God.
And in their time,
of precious communion,
the Ephod was laid aside,
as the nations of promise,
built a golden glistening calf,
they could see.

Moses heard the cry,
as God shed a tear.

Jealousy raged,
in the vibrant foundations,
of Heaven.
And Moses cried out,
for the souls of the lost,
as iniquity reigned once again,
in the earth.

Stones of fire,
shown again,
in the crowns of the kings,
that ruled over the nations.
Crowns of the righteous,
killed by the crowds of the wicked,
coveting the beauty,
of the precious glowing stones.

Then, in that last day,
as the Mystery Babylon,
walks the corrupted streets,
of earth,
no one will buy her merchandise.
Not the gold or silver,
precious stones or fine linen,
not the horses, chariots or slaves,
not the souls of men.

Finally the nations will see,
that the soul cannot share,
the beauty meant for the eye.
Beauty meant to be enjoyed,
to enhance, to appreciate.

The stones of fire,
a wedding gift,
from the God of creation,
changed into a god,
by the lusts of man.

Gazing on their fiery beauty,
we wonder at the value,
the prestige,
and forget the covenant of love,
for which they stand.

The birth of a child,
the birth of a nation,
a covenant of love,
sealed by the signet,
of a fiery stone.

A marriage of two people,
two nations,
two entities;
destined to find perfection,
in the confines of Heaven.

So they wait,
undefiled,
in the third Heaven,
where angels and cherubim,
commune with,
the one true God.

Jerusalem Lieth Waste

Nehemiah 1 – 2 – 3

Jerusalem lieth waste,
Her children are scattered,
Her children's children wander aimlessly,
Searching for any sign of hope.
The fountains have lost their beauty,
The waters are bitter.
The walls of the city have no gates,
Where the gates once were, there are no doors,
All have fallen away,
None have taken the time to restore and repair.
Into the valley they travel,
Past the dunghill, the remnant of past life,
Past the pool where the animals find rest.
Between two mountains they are tossed about,
A mountain of good, secure but foreign;
A mountain of evil, exciting and lurid.
In the valley they wait,
Walking to and fro, from mountain to mountain,
Tasting of the ambience of each,
Looking for one who will care enough,
To restore them.
At the walls stand a handful of Saints,
Each trying to decide whether to help,
Or to let others live as they will.

Should they reach out to another's child,
Chance the rebuke and scorn,
Can they make a difference,
Or become a passing trend,
Soon forgotten.
Rebuilding the walls will take so much time,
Establishing the gates difficult,
Placing doors means people to watch them,
People that discern good and evil,
People of integrity that will not compromise.
Jerusalem lieth waste,
Her children's children have not been taught,
Her children's children's wounds have not been tended,
Her children's children wander aimlessly,
Searching for hope.
A handful of Saints make a decision,
This restoration will take many years,
This restoration will be painful,
This restoration will make a difference,
This restoration will set a standard.
I pick up the first stone and set it in place,
Then another and another,
I hear the laughter and the scorn,
It feeds my intensity.
As the walls strengthen and the doors are set,
The children wander back;
They find security, soundness, protection;
They find safety, boundaries, goals;
They find hope,
They find peace.

Storyteller

"But this shall be the covenant that I will make with the house of Israel; After those days, saith the Lord, I will put my law in their inward parts, and write it in their hearts; and will be their God, and they shall be my people." Jeremiah 31:33

From the first time I saw the Storyteller and was told the story behind it I have wanted one. Storytellers, carved by Native Americans, have one large person at the center, eyes closed and mouth open, and lots of little people all around most sitting upon the large person; listening.

In the Native American culture, the Storyteller was usually the oldest person in the tribe, male or female, who taught the history of the tribe to the children. The history of the tribe was passed from generation to generation by the stories the Storyteller painted.

This little statue has always reminded me of the early Jewish culture, where fathers sat and taught their sons the lineage of their family, the words of God (the Old Testament), and primarily the Torah. The only written reminders of history, for thousands of years, were the scrolls kept in the synagogue and read by the priests to the men of age. It was the duty of the men to teach the family and to help the sons memorize the words on the scrolls.

In today's culture we are spoiled by inexpensive Bibles, study tools, computer software, audio and video tapes. Bible memorization, other than in Sunday school classrooms, is uncommon, and essentially, not desired.

Why memorize something you can retrieve in a moment's notice? The answer - relationship. Intimacy with God is never accomplished through a keyboard and a hard-drive. Intimacy with God is accomplished by knowing His story, knowing it, meditating on it, sharing it (storytelling), by putting it deep within your and your children's hearts.

Instant coffee, instant food, instant scriptures. Lord, remind me always of the preciousness of Your Word that I may never take it for granted. Remind me to study and read, day and night, that Your Word will be etched in my heart.

A Chose Vessel . . .

"And the vessel that he made of clay was marred in the hand of the
potter: so he made it again another vessel, as seemed good to the
potter to make it." Jeremiah 18:4
"Hath not the potter power over the clay, of the same lump to make
one vessel unto honour, and another unto dishonour?" Romans 9:21

Painted with Love,
Fired with Patience,
Filled with Righteousness,
Kissed by the Grace of God.
I am a Chosen Vessel.

Sweet Fragrance

"I will accept you with your sweet savour, when I bring you out from the people, and gather you out of the countries wherein ye have been scattered; and I will be sanctified in you before the heathen." Ezekiel 20:41

I love flowers. I could study the simple beauty of a flower for hours - breathing in the gentle aroma that lifts from the petals. I am completely convinced that when God created the Heavens and the earth He knew I was coming and created flowers just for me!

I most enjoy the age-old garden variety flower; the one with bugs and bees. The kind you can smell without having to bend down and stick your nose in. I grow them in pots at home, as well as in my office. Being blessed with an office window and a door to the outside, I now enjoy the fresh color every time I have to deliver a memo. God is so good!

This last Mother's Day I was given a carnation by a local restaurant. It was a beautiful peach color. It immediately brought back memories of buying carnations from the "Flower Children" in the 70's and 80's as they held their street corner stations. I quickly buried my nose in the cool petals but was surprised and dismayed at the absence of its sweet perfume. There was no aroma - no sweetness.

A few days later I was given a rose boutonniere, left over from an awards presentation. The leaves were perfectly formed, the bud slightly opened - the rich red petals were awesome - but no aroma.

As beautiful as these two flowers were, there was a hollowness, an incompleteness, like a peach without flavor, or a lamp without light. The first flower I thought was an oddity, but the second was more than coincidence.

All that week, as I passed retail flower shops, I would stop to smell the flowers - NOTHING!! "Lord," I prayed, "where is the sweetness You created with this gift? Why is it gone?"

The answer came as simply as asked, "There is no fragrance without the sun."

These plants had been grown in greenhouses, under artificial lights, in special climate controlled conditions. No warmth of the sun, or cool of the night. No rain from Heaven, just processed city water. No fragrance.

We, too, are like greenhouse flowers. We can be beautiful to look upon, and give the "Impression" of sweetness from a distance, but without the Son, kissing us every day with His soul feeding Word, we have no sweet fragrance. Impressions only last a moment, but beauty, blessed with sweetness, will remain a pleasant memory for a lifetime.

The Bible refers to our praise and sacrifice as a sweet savor, rising up to the nostrils of God; an eternal pleasure in God's memory. Lord, let me always be a sweet savor in Your thoughts. Remind me, daily, that without the Son, and the gift He gave, there will be no fragrance.

Jerusalem

"Happy art thou, O Israel: who is like unto thee, O people saved by the Lord, the shield of thy help, and who is the sword of thy excellency! and thine enemies shall be found liars unto thee; and thou shalt tread upon their high places." Deuteronomy. 33:29

Mighty in power,
Stand up Jerusalem,
Born of a King,
Born of the light.
Draw in the children
From the nations, Jerusalem,
Strengthened in love,
Pure in sight.
Carry the shield
The sword,
And the armor,
Carry the word,
The truth
And the light.
Hold them up high,
The enemy beckons,
Ready to go,
Ready to fight.

There You Are Jesus

"I am crucified with Christ: nevertheless I live; yet not I, but Christ liveth in me: and the life which I now live in the flesh I live by the faith of the Son of God, who loved me, and gave himself for me."

Galatians 2:20

What happens when innocence is lost? Like a fresh new flower, ripped from the plant, first we wilt, then harden, then we crumble and are blown away.

I love movies, especially children's movies. One of my favorite is Peter Pan, the version where Robin Williams plays Peter. At the beginning of the movie, he doesn't realize that he's Peter. He's lost his innocence. He'd lost touch with what things in life are truly important. He believes the tale of Peter Pan is something made up and passed down in stories from generation to generation.

Movies, as they are, overlook the logical (that's what I love about them) and Robin Williams ends up in Neverland with the lost boys. The lost boys try desperately to convince him of who he is and teach him how to be a child again. Everything in Neverland is completely dependent upon imagination. They wouldn't even have food, drink or sustenance without a good, active imagination.

The lost boys are finally successful at helping Peter find his innocence again and let go of the stresses and frustrations of schedules, bills and responsibilities of the real world. At one point in the movie, one of the lost boys walks up to Robin Williams, looks deep into his eyes and says, "Oh, there you are Peter." A revelation of innocence returned.

This sequence always reminds me of my Christian faith. So many times we're caught up in the stress and frustrations of schedules and appointments and trying to please so many in so little time, that we lose the miracle and the innocence of working in ministry. Our innocence is dependent upon our faith. Sometimes we allow the enemy to convince us that by striving we work the good work, when in fact, it is by faith and the leading of the Holy Spirit that we accomplish everything that God has called us to do; without the loss of innocence.

I look hopefully to the time when I can casually enjoy all of those around me, without worrying about where I should be, lest I fall behind (again!!). I look forward to the day when I will be filled with faith to the point of complete peace and serenity. When someone, perhaps a child, will look deep into my eyes and say, "Oh, there you are Jesus." When the Jesus in me will shine past my many earthly flaws.

Jesus, may I always hear and obey your voice. That the innocence, birthed in faith, will always be the most obvious attribute in my life.

Release

"And all this assembly shall know that the Lord saveth not with sword and spear: for the battle is the Lord's, and he will give you into our hands." 1 Samuel 17:47

Rise up my bride, soil not your gown.
Release the sword from your delicate fingers.
Rest with peace as I stand guard.
Your war is finished, the battle finally won.
Now the chamber waits with sweet fragrances
Of sanctioned prayers,
Washed clean with bottled tears.
Step up with me,
Safe within my arms,
In the place you never doubted would come.
Today we stand as one,
Faith upon Faith,
Truth within Truth,
Life into Eternity.

Tiny Flame

No man, when he hath lighted a candle, putteth it in a secret place, neither under a bushel, but on a candlestick, that they which come in may see the light. Luke 11:33

Being burdened down by the flu on New Year's Eve 1999 kept me home from the outstanding event our church had been preparing for the previous 4 months. I sent my prayers for my church family and the events they worked so hard on – then I laid back down and prayed for relief from the symptoms I'd been fighting for 2 ½ days.

The year 2000 was about to become a reality, 2000 years since the death of our precious savior – 2000 years of salvation by faith, by grace, by the blood of Christ. 2000 years.

We've come from traveling by foot, to traveling by jet plane. From writing on the bark of a tree with the juice of berries, to computers and the internet. From never traveling farther than 30 miles from where we were born, to the moon, mars and beyond.

We come from a way of life where our entire days were surrounded by the teaching of the ways of the Biblical Fathers, to the days where people walked with Christ – God made flesh to the time where it is difficult to work 10 minutes of prayer into our busy daily schedules. We have advanced our civilization in the last 100 years at a pace that has outreached any imagination the early pioneers could have had. We have created, and created, and created at such a rapid pace that we have left ourselves little time to remember, let alone thank, the creator of all.

I prepared my candle and matches, just in case the Y2K doomsayers were correct and I needed to travel from one end of the house to the other in total darkness. I lit the candle and realized how I've always been drawn to the tiny flame. It has always intrigued me how lighting a candle during the day gives off so little light, but at night, when all other light has been extinguished, that one tiny flame can illuminate an enormous room.

Drawing close to the flame you can feel the warmth that it emits. A warmth far beyond its tiny reach. This light and warmth draws me together with those who have shared this very moment for hundreds and thousands of years. Long before the birth of Christ. Before Moses and the burning bush, that burned and yet wasn't consumed. Long before Pharaoh and Noah.

A light and a warmth that comforted Adam and Eve, expelled from Paradise, sent into a land of unknown sounds, shadows and total darkness – caused from being apart from God. I envision their being drawn to the flame, like the many times they drew near to God's glory; warm and comforting.

Like that tiny flame, I wonder what part I play in the spiritual darkness that has spread across the world. Can the small flame that burns inside me, lit by the Holy Spirit and fed by the anointing, create enough light to show others the way to Christ? Can that flame generate enough warmth to draw the confused to a place of comfort and understanding? Lord, I pray that as long as I remain on this earth, may I always share the light that's within me. Help me to feed the hungry and comfort the comfortless. Let me always remember that the reason I have been placed upon this earth is to praise and give all glory to You!

Oh, Come Now

"But I have said unto you, Ye shall inherit their land, and I will give it
unto you to possess it, a land that floweth with milk and honey: I am
the Lord your God, which have separated you from other people."
Leviticus 20:24

In the challenge of tomorrow,
The world can be so cold,
We are called to shine as beacons,
A task not easily done.
Yet we walk with pride and victory,
'Cause we know what's to come,
As we're singing hallelujah,
Oh, Lord, we're coming home.
Oh, come now,
Sweet Spirit,
Sweet Honey from above,
Precious Bread,
That's never gone.
Bring Rivers,
Of Water,
To lead me along,
As the Spirit takes me home.

To Know

As thou knowest not what is the way of the spirit, nor how the bones
do grow in the womb of her that is with child: even so thou knowest
not the works of God who maketh all. Ecclesiastes 11:5
The wind bloweth where it listeth, and thou hearest the sound thereof,
but canst not tell whence it cometh, and whither it goeth: so is every
one that is born of the Spirit.
John 3:8

At the breath of dawn
I raise my life to You.

I feel your warmth,
caressing the weary lines
that etch and pull
at the curves of my face.

Your light tenderly penetrates
the closed lids
of my eyes,
beckoning me to see,
far past the visible realm.

I raise myself up,
straight and tall,
pleading to you for the strength
I once had
of my own ability.

My own strength fails,
as it always has,
but Your strength overcomes
my weakness
as I step out for You.

I remain in sweet communion,
our spirits touch through
the gift of Your precious Spirit.
I absorb and regenerate
from the power of joining with You.
Your anointing oil pours
from the cup of Your desires
to the hope of my will.

I see what you have called me to,
but understand not.
I touch the oil that flows
down my garments
and wonder "Why"?

The oil glistens on my fingertips
as I take it to its appointed work.
I question and doubt,
every step of the way,
at why I was chosen for this work;
whether I could truly
make a difference.

As I reach the appointed place,
I reach out and touch the life

I've been sent to heal.

The anointing and the Spirit become one,
coursing through this vessel.

The Spirit speaks forth
as virtue flows out
through these fingertips
and into another called of God.

After the evening passes
and the shadows of doubt diminish
I return to the dawn
to seek You once again.

I so desire to know You,
to understand the plans
You've set in motion.
a plan that only you
can comprehend.
Forgive me, Lord, in the dusk of doubt.
Help me to know that
my greatest mission
is to carry forth the touch
You have put in my hand,
And to take the steps,
You have placed in my feet.

Help me to realize that
all I need to know,
all I need to understand,

is that every move I make
is completely in Your will.

Fallen Fruit

"But the fruit of the Spirit is love, joy, peace, longsuffering, gentleness, goodness, faith, Meekness, temperance: against such there is no law."
Galatians 5:22-23

Stepping up to an office,
Stationed by God,
I stand in the valley of change.
Casting down yesterday's garments,
Putting on the mantle of righteousness,
Sending out the proclamation,
The ways of the past are cut off,
Tomorrow we walk anew.
Many are the voices of comfort,
That come against me.
My shield drops in disappointment.
The arrows of discontent,
And false accusation wound me,
Causing my fruit to be pierced,
And fall down around my feet.
Then, I recognize the voice,
Not the voice of the brethren,
Only the vessel,
Confused for a season.
It is the voice of the enemy.
I cast off hurt as I raise my shield.
Many fruit have fallen,
My branches are broken and splintered,
But next to the wounds are buds of hope,

Watered by the words of the spirit,
Preparing the branches for an abundance,
Of new fruit.

Troubled Water

"For an angel went down at a certain season into the pool, and troubled the water: whosoever then first after the troubling of the water stepped in was made whole of whatsoever disease he had. The impotent man answered him, Sir, I have no man, when the water is troubled, to put me into the pool: but while I am coming, another steppeth down before me. John 5:4 & 7

I can feel it -
the shaking,
the stirring,
inside.
The angels
have troubled the water,
deep within me.
Who will help me,
draw close to the pool,
where pure love can heal?
Where the Glory of God,
lights the dark recesses of doubt.
If I move quickly,
toward the call of God,
the desperate corners,
I find to hide in,
will be purged and cleansed,
and my Spirit,
will be set free,

to soar above the circumstances,
my soul calls hopeless.
Who will take the chance,
of entering into my world,
and carry me down,
to the healing pool,
where Spirit and soul,
come together?
Who will lay their life open,
to care - to hurt - to lift?
Could it be you?

Moab is My Washpot

Psalm 60 and Psalm 108

I have been set between two warring factions,
Each is dear to my heart.
I stand between the two and push each back,
Trying in the physical to do that,
Which only the spiritual can change.
The anger and violence that explodes is frightening,
It cannot continue - it must not.
One faction leaves in rage,
Tainting the lives of those left behind.
I grieve.
I grieve in travail that seemingly,
Cannot be quenched.
I pray and clean my house,
I pray and stand in faith,
I pray and wait for my miracle,
It is taking so long.
"Moab is my washpot," says God,
my thorn, of incestuous birth,
and my cleansing bowl.
Moab is my washpot,
A chosen outsider that I love,
With all of my heart.
I long to draw him close,
Yet he has pushed me far away.
I kneel before God,
Cleansing my past,

Cleansing my generations,
Cleansing the ground on which I stand,
Cleansing the future for my family to come.
As I prepare a new path,
A new home, a new way,
The heaviness of anger and grief lift.
When my loved one returns,
Peace will overcome turmoil,
Love will overcome rage.
There will be much pain to be healed,
There will be times of testing,
Times of patience,
Times of re-washing and cleansing,
Times of reconciliation.
I bless God for the times that Moab rose up,
For we had a mere existence,
An acceptance of the way things were,
Things that were not right.
Without Moab, things might never have changed,
Now God can work His will,
In drawing us together,
The way we should have always been,
But couldn't find the way.
Thank you God, for the trial of Moab.

Wax Museum

(The Eyes of the Hopelessly Dead)
"The light of the body is the eye: therefore when thine eye is single, thy whole body also is full of light; but when thine eye is evil, thy body also is full of darkness." Luke 11:34

Vacations are interesting entities. They are times when you spend money you know better than to spend and visit places that you may have only had a vague interest in previously.

In our family, vacations are a valued commodity that arrive only once every 3 - 4 years. It's a time when we have saved and set aside so that we can travel off for a day or two and leave everything behind for someone else to care for. This year was our year of VACATION!!

We had been given our hotel room as a gift and part of that gift included tickets to the Movieland Wax Museum. None of us had ever been to a wax museum - however, none of us had ever really been over-enthusiastic about going to one either. But, it was vacation! A time to see something new! A time to . . . well, you know.

At first, I was intrigued by the replicas; life-size dolls, the exact size of a famous movie star, wearing the original costume from a movie or an article of clothing from the movie star's personal wardrobe - or so they claim.

The tour began with the older movies. What took me by surprise was the size of the stars. The women were so tiny, petite (to compensate for the 20 extra pounds the camera add, I suspect). Jean Harlow, Bette Davis, Kathryn Hepburn - all movie greats, up close and personal.

Then there were the men. Characters that loomed so large on the screen were trim young men, not much taller than myself. The illusion of grandeur diminished. The overwhelming feeling of awe was reduced.

They were just people. People who struggled with self-esteem and the pressures of fame. People, just like me, who tried to juggle work and family and (prayerfully) devotions.

As I continued the tour I recognized depression setting over me. Why, Lord? What are you showing me that I can't see?

"Look at them," He said, "carefully."

I began to look into the faces - past the aging clothing, the dusty sets, the fading make-up, and a few missing fingers. I stood in one spot and turned a full circle, looking carefully into the eyes of the replicas.

"There's nothing, Lord, nothing!"

And that was it! Deep in the eyes was the absence of the soul. They were exact replicas of the bodies of men - void of love, hate, joy, dreams and visions. It was a morgue of dead bodies, dressed up to entertain people. I walked through the "horror" section and felt nothing. Even with the sound tracks playing in the background of some of the sets, there was nothing. The eyes were dead and blank. There were no demons, no tormented souls, no hate, no raging insanity. They were the eyes of the hopelessly dead.

After leaving the museum I searched the face of every person I saw. The daily anguish, joy and stresses were there. It slowly relieved my depression. It gave me new hope and a fresh battleground. For in the tormented eyes there is hope for salvation. In joy there is peace and encouragement for tomorrow.

No matter what the tormented soul is screaming out through the eyes - as long as there is life, there is an opportunity for Jesus to enter in.

Lord, let me always remember that every face I see could belong to a soul of little time. Give me the courage to change the demons that dance in those eyes, before they become the eyes of the hopelessly dead.

Majesty

"He that dwelleth in the secret place of the most High shall abide under the shadow of the Almighty.I will say of the Lord, He is my refuge and my fortress: my God; in him will I trust. Surely he shall deliver thee from the snare of the fowler, and from the noisome pestilence. He shall cover thee with his feathers, and under his wings shalt thou trust: his truth shall be thy shield and buckler." Psalm 91:1-4

In the shadows of your wings,
We humbly come before Your throne.
Letting praise and worship ring,
Our words of love to You alone.
Majesty, Majesty.
Gentle whispers draw our prayers,
In loving arms He holds us near.
Precious moments linger there,
A refuge, safe, above all fear.
Majesty, Majesty.
As the gentle spirit flows,
He pulls away the tempered walls.
The new tender heart He shows,
The world in splendor as He calls.
Majesty, Majesty.

Inferno

That the trial of your faith, being much more precious than of gold that perisheth, though it be tried with fire, might be found unto praise and honour and glory at the appearing of Jesus Christ: 1 Peter 1:7

Here I stand,
Safe in the hand of God,
Kissed by a gentle breeze,
Cooled by the living water,
Of the Spirit.
All around me rages an inferno,
To my right, to my left,
Directly in my path.
The bowels of hell,
Threatening death,
Always testing my faith,
But held away,
By my closest friend, my savior.
Here I stand,
And here I will stay,
Until I hear the voice of God,
Directing my steps,
To reach the lost,
With His precious love.

Epilogue

Intimate time with Jesus has a precious fragrance that is so sweet it cannot be described. The deepest, most hidden portion of your soul softens and drifts gently up to be touched and healed by the Master. You become as an innocent child again. The days seem brighter, the evenings more vibrant. Even the smallest, seemingly insignificant things bring on new meaning and value. You see the grace and gift of God in every situation. It is truly a wondrous place to be.

About the Author

Linda is the Founder and President of Shiloh Spiritual Growth Ministries, an Ordained Pastor, Music Minister, Teacher, Counselor, Mentor and Watercolor Artist. Linda received her BA in Theology through Biltmore Bible University in Phoenix, AZ. Linda has written 3 books of reflection and is currently writing her 4th: Book 1 is titled Moments With The Master, A Reflective Time. Book 2 is titled A Walk To Gethsemane, Touching The Master's Hand. Book 3 is titled The Emmaus Road, Sharing A Heart Of Faith, which is currently being formatted. Book 4 is titled, The Damascus Road, A Journey Through Ephesians, which is currently in the writing process.

Linda writes Inspirational Literature that helps the reader find a deep, intimate relationship with Jesus Christ. Linda developed the curriculum for RiverFire University in Phoenix, AZ and is currently teaching Christian study classes in Northern Arizona.

"Blessed *be* the LORD my strength, which teacheth my hands to war, *and* my fingers to fight:" *Psalms 144:1 (KJV)*